Prison or Paradise?

PRISON OR PARADISE?

The New Religious Cults

A. James Rudin
Marcia R. Rudin

Fortress Press
Philadelphia

Published by Fortress Press
Philadelphia
COPYRIGHT © 1980 BY A. JAMES RUDIN AND MARCIA R. RUDIN

First printing June 1980
Second printing September 1980

Library of Congress Cataloging in Publication Data

Rudin, Arnold James.
  Prison or Paradise?

  Bibliography: p.
  1. Cults—United States. I. Rudin, Marcia R.,
1940- joint author. II. Title.
BL2530.U6R82   291'.0973   80-10210
ISBN 0-8006-0637-X

8844I80   Printed in the United States of America   1-637

CONTENTS

Introduction   7
Acknowledgments   11

Chapter 1 • The Cult Boom   13

What Are the New Religious Cults?—How Many Cults Are
There?—Why Are Today's Cults Different?—The Religious
Cults Are Wealthy—Guarding Against Complacency—
Characteristics of the Cults—Are the New Cults Dangerous?

Chapter 2 • The Major Religious Cults   31

The Unification Church—The International Society for
Krishna Consciousness—The Way International—Tony and
Susan Alamo Christian Foundation—The Divine Light
Mission—Church of Armageddon/Love Family—Body
of Christ—The Children of God—The Church of
Scientology

Chapter 3 • **The Target Is You!
Who Joins and Why?**   97

Who Joins the Cults—The Religious Background of
Cultists—Is There a Typical Cult Member?—Why Are Cults
So Attractive Now?—Cults Provide a Caring Community

Chapter 4 • **Countering the Cults**   119

Legal Options for Parents—Deprogramming—Is
Deprogramming Legal?—First Amendment Issues—Using
the Legal System to Counter the Cults—Preventive
Remedies—Former Members and Others Sue the Cults—
Other Ways to Counter the Cults—Guidelines for Parents—
What Are the Problems of Former Cult Members?

Chapter 5 • **Can Christianity and Judaism
Meet the Challenge of the Cults**   147

Suggested Reading List   151
Counter-Cult Organizations   153
Index   155

INTRODUCTION

Our first contact with the new religious cults began in the mid 1970s with a large number of telephone calls and letters from anguished parents. The disturbing stories they told were almost identical: a young son or daughter suddenly leaves the family, drops out of work or school, disappears into a new religious group, and blindly serves, even worships, the strong charismatic leader of the group. In many cases, all communication between parent and child had ended, and when there was contact, the new cult member often spoke in either dull, robot-like monosyllables or in an almost strange language filled with new terms and concepts. In every case the parent's cry from the heart was the same: "Help me find my child! Tell what you know about the group my child has joined! Who is Rev. Moon, Swami Prabhupada, Victor Wierwille, Susan Alamo, Maharaj Ji, Paul Erdman, David (Moses) Berg, L. Ron Hubbard?

We were profoundly touched by the calls for assistance and information, but at the beginning we were unable to respond adequately. Although both of us have been professionally trained in the study of religion and philosophy, the sudden rise of the new religious cults caught us (and millions of others) unaware. But as the calls and letters mounted in number and intensity, we turned our attention to the cults, and our initial discoveries were unsettling.

We immersed ourselves in the cults' teaching materials. We familiarized ourselves with the doctrines and life-styles of the various cults. We spoke with cult members, ex-members, parents, as well as with a host of religious, medical, legal, educational, and political leaders. We talked with deprogrammers and those who are opposed to deprogramming. The more we learned the more disquieted we became.

Because of our concern about the cults we have spoken before many audiences in the United States and Canada on the subject. Many who heard us were openly skeptical of the disturbing message we brought. They often disputed our contention that religious cults pose serious problems for society and many of the young people we addressed failed to see the difference between these cults and established religious groups. But after nearly every public appearance one or two embarrassed and distraught people, representing every racial, religious, ethnic, and economic group, would come up to us to confess that they had a family member or friend in a cult and to seek information about it. These desperate people urged us to continue our work, and their stories confirmed the validity of our research and findings. Alas, after the Jonestown tragedy in November, 1978, much of the skepticism and doubt disappeared.

Following the People's Temple massacre, some optimists believed the cult phenomenon would come to an end. Clearly, this has not happened; indeed, it is our belief that the cults are stronger than ever.

In this book we seek to reach a larger audience in order to alert people to the dangers of the cults, and to offer some effective ways of legally countering them. We have quite consciously limited ourselves to nine of the major *religious* cults.

However, we are well aware that some extremist political organizations and some human-potential groups exhibit many of the same negative characteristics we attribute to the nine cults described in this volume. Nor are we unaware of the duplicity and the deceptive methods practiced by certain "Hebrew Christian" groups. These practices have been publicly condemned by responsible Christian and Jewish leadership. Although we do not believe that these are "hard-core" cults as we define the term, they are, nonetheless, a continuing source of concern to all those who are committed to the integrity and authenticity of both Judaism and Christianity. We have, elsewhere,* expressed our views on the "Hebrew Christians."

The opinions in this book are our own and do not reflect the policies or positions of the American Jewish Committee.

Finally, this book is a delayed response to all those calls and letters. We are only sorry that it took so long to answer you. . .

A. JAMES RUDIN   MARCIA R. RUDIN

*Present Tense, Summer 1977, published by the American Jewish Committee, New York City, pp. 17-26.

ACKNOWLEDGMENTS

Our research could not have been completed without the splendid assistance of many colleagues at the American Jewish Committee. We express special thanks also to Lillian Block and her staff at the Religious News Service. We are grateful to Berenice Hoffman who helped us develop the project from its inception. Special appreciation goes to Ingalill Hjelm, our editor. We also acknowledge the indispensable help we received from parents of cult members, from former members, and from cult followers themselves. We give special thanks to Ex-Members Against Moon.

Finally, the patience award must go to our daughters, Eve and Jennifer, who cheerfully endured long hours of parental involvement with this book.

Chapter 1

THE CULT BOOM

A brilliant Ivy League college graduate writes his parents a short cryptic note informing them he has found a new life with the Children of God. They never see their child again.

On Manhattan's West Side a former opera coach named Oric Bovar proclaims himself Jesus Christ and attracts followers from the entertainment world who contribute large sums of money to support his cult. When one of his young followers dies Bovar prays over the body for its resurrection in an apartment for three months. Finally health officials intervene and bury the body. On April 14, 1977, Oric Bovar jumps to his death from the window of his tenth-floor West-End Avenue apartment.

Dr. Joseph Jeffers builds a $200,000 pyramid called the Temple of Yahoshua 100 miles southwest of St. Louis, Missouri. Jeffers, who claims he is the Son of God, is the founder and leader of a religion called Yahwism.

In November, 1978, 911 men, women, and children, members of the Reverend Jim Jones's Guyana jungle utopia, Jonestown, die by drinking a Kool-Aid and cyanide mixture or are shot to death by guards.

What Are the New Religious Cults?

What are these new religious cults? Are the cults a new phenomenon, or are they similar to religious cults that have always existed? How many new groups are there? How many members have they attracted? Are they a fad that will pass, or are they a permanent part of the worldwide religious scene? Are they dangerous, or are they a welcome addition to religious and to cultural pluralism?

Sociologists define cults as deviant groups which exist in a state of tension with society. They do not evolve or break away from other religions, as do religious sects, but, rather, offer something new and different. Although by definition cults conflict with "the establishment," there are degrees of conflict: the more total the commitment the cults demand from their followers, the more hostility they meet from society.

There have always been religious cults, particularly in unstable and troubled times such as ours. For example, the Roman Empire, which allowed great freedom of religion, was deluged with apocalyptic movements that sprang from the meeting of Eastern and Western cultures. Throughout history there have always been people, both young and old, who have sought personal fulfillment, peace, mystical experience, and religious salvation through such fringe groups.

Today's religious cults, however, are different from those of the past for several reasons. First of all, there has never in recorded history been such a proliferation of cults. The signs of this cult "boom" are everywhere. Bulletin boards on hundreds of college campuses advertise a smorgasbord of religious options. Both conventional newspapers and magazines and "alternative life-style" publications carry advertisements. Cult members recruit and solicit contributions in stores, on street corners, and in public parks, in tourist centers and airports. Everywhere one hears stories of children, brothers and sisters, nieces and nephews, older parents, or friends who become members of one of these groups. Ministers, priests, and rabbis hear desperate pleas for help, as do the major Jewish and Christian organizations.

How Many Cults Are There?

Although we do not know the precise number of these cults, we do know that it is large and that the numbers are growing. After an extensive study, Drs. Egon Mayer and Laura Kitch, sociologists at Brooklyn College, concluded that since 1965 more than thirteen hundred new religious groups have appeared in America. Other observers estimate that there are between one and three thousand such groups in the United States alone. Not all are large and well-known. Some last only a short time. Many of these cults are simply the personal creations of their founders and do not outlive them, such as that of Oric Bovar, which came to an end with his suicide.

Just as it is difficult to know how many cults there are, so, too, it is difficult to estimate the number of people involved in them. Accurate membership records are not available. The membership figures the cults release are usually highly inflated in order to appear larger and to give the impression that their growth is more rapid than may really be the case. Cult critics who overreact in their concern may inadvertently inflate the figures or may underestimate them. Cult members tend to float from one group to another with the consequence that one individual may be counted in membership figures several times. Dr. Marc Galanter, a psychiatrist at Yeshiva University's Albert Einstein Medical School in New York City who, along with Richard Rabkin and Judith Rabkin, studied the Unification Church in late 1978, discovered that 90 percent of its members had had a previous involvement with another cult, confirming that there is a good deal of "shopping around" within these groups. Some experts estimate there are three hundred thousand cult adherents. Flo Conway and Jim Siegelman, authors of *Snapping,* assert there are perhaps as many as 3 million past and present cult members in America alone.* Dr. Margaret Thaler Singer, a psychiatrist on the staff of the Wright Institute at Berkeley, California, and the University of California in San Fransisco and a cult expert, who counsels former cult members, agrees that there are 2 to 3 million people in these groups.

Never before have religious cults been so geographically widespread. They are in every area of the United States, in every major city and on college campuses throughout the nation. They have spread to Canada and to Western Europe—Great Britain, France, Holland, Denmark, Italy, and West Germany—where governments are alarmed about their rapid growth. There are cult centers also in Asia, Africa, South America, Israel, Australia, and New Zealand.

Today's cultists are trained in the latest methods of group dynamics and "Madison Avenue" public relations, advertising, and media-manipulation techniques. They bring great enthusiasm to their work and make certain that all members are highly visible and effective missionizers. This dedication heightens their efficiency well beyond their numbers.

Why Are Today's Cults Different?

One of the major factors which set the new religious cults off from those of the past is their use of new, specific, and highly sophisticated techniques which successfully manipulate thought and behavior of new cult members. Hundreds of former cult members testify this is so in court proceedings, public information hearings concerning the cults, magazine and newspaper interviews, and counseling sessions. Psychiatrists and other professionals who counsel former cultists confirm this. These techniques include constant repetition of doctrine, application of intense peer pressure, manipulation of diet so that critical faculties are adversely affected, deprivation of sleep, lack of privacy and time for reflection, complete break with past life, reduction of outside stimulation and influ-

*Conway, Flo and Siegelman, Jim, *Snapping: America's Epidemic of Sudden Personality Change* (New York: J. B. Lippincott Company, 1978), p. 12.

ences, the skillful use of ritual to heighten mystical experience, and the invention of new vocabulary and the manipulation of language to narrow down the range of experience and construct a new reality. Psychiatrists and counselors who treat former cult members say their emotional and intellectual responses have been severely curtailed. Dr. John G. Clark, Jr., Associate Clinical Professor of Psychiatry at Massachusetts General Hospital-Harvard Medical School, who has worked with former cult members for the past six and one-half years says:

> They appear to have become rather dull and their style and range of expression limited and stereotyped. They are animated only when discussing their group and its beliefs. They rapidly lose a knowledge of current events. When stressed even a little, they become defensive and inflexible and retreat into numbing cliches. Their written or spoken expression loses metaphor, irony, and the broad use of vocabulary. Their humor is without mirth.*

Observers believe some cults use hypnosis and posthypnotic suggestion.

These methods can bring about a complete personality transformation. The cult leader can mold the recruit's new beliefs and personality according to his desires so the new adherent will have total commitment to the group. This can happen very quickly, sometimes within a period of weeks.

Authors Conway and Siegelman believe that in most cults there is "a single moment of conversion and transformation," which they term "snapping." This moment is "induced in the course of a cult ritual or therapeutic technique that is deftly orchestrated to create the experience of a momentous psychic breakthrough." After this experience the person is highly vulnerable to suggestion. The cults follow up the process by

*Testimony of Dr. John G. Clark, Jr., Information Meeting on the Cult Phenomenon in the United States, Washington, D.C., February 5, 1979. Transcript reprinted by American Family Foundation, Inc., Lexington, Massachusetts, pp. 41-42.

chanting, meditation, speaking in tongues, or other mental exercises which reinforce the effects of the sudden psychic experience and also act as mechanisms to stifle future doubts. The results of this expert thought manipulation can be neutralized only with great difficulty. In some cases these changes are permanent.

The Religious Cults Are Wealthy

Today's religious cults are unique also because of their great wealth. They charge high fees for classes or lectures and sometimes actually take over their members' financial assets. They own extensive property, operate lucrative and diversified businesses, and skillfully extract millions of dollars every year from the public by solicitations. Their incomes are taxexempt. The People's Temple had over $10 million in various bank accounts at the time of the mass suicides and murders in Guyana. Ex Unification Church official Allen Tate Wood estimates that movement's income is over $200 million per year.

Money buys power. Some cults can afford to hire the best legal minds to help them fight their opponents. They sue journalists who write about them and campaign against legislation that aims to curb their activities. The Unification Church hires top journalists and columnists to write for its newspaper, *News World,* which offers a widespread platform for its political viewpoint. Critics accuse the Unification Church of using its great wealth to influence United States Government policy.

Money can also purchase respectability. The cults are changing their tactics. They are less flamboyant and no longer hire Madison Square Garden or the Houston Astrodome for rallies. They are taking many adherents off the streets and putting them into "white-collar" jobs. Cultists who are visible to the public dress in a better manner than they did in the past so that outsiders will think the group is less eccentric and therefore less dangerous. Many Hare Krishna members, for example, now wear wigs and conventional clothing when they solicit on the streets rather than their exotic Indian garb. The

Unification Church employs reknowned theologians to teach at its seminary and to lecture on the group's behalf. It "dialogues" with Evangelical Christians and desires conversations with other religious groups. It seeks the academic world's stamp of approval by inviting over four hundred fifty prominent academicians to annual conferences sponsored by a Unification-Church organization, ICUS (International Conference on the Unity of Science), which pays for their travel expenses and large honoraria. Some academics are flattered by the invitations, while others refuse to attend the controversial meetings because of the Unification Church connection.

Because of their vast wealth and the power and respectability money can buy the contemporary cults are not merely a passing fad. They are not simply temporary way stations for those who may "be into" something else next year, as some hope. They are a permanent and rapidly growing part of the worldwide religious and cultural scene.

Guarding Against Complacency

Although the cults are a very real presence on the religious and cultural scene this does not mean that we must be complacent about them. They want people to get used to them, to become resigned to their existence, to tire of worrying and stop fighting against them. They want to be perceived as "new religious movements" rather than as "cults," a negative label which implies that they are at odds with society. They liken themselves to other religious movements which were previously considered radical and which are now, after the passage of time, old, established, and accepted groups. Unification Church officials often compare their legal difficulties and negative public image to the past harassment of the Mormon Church, implying that just as the Mormons were once considered outsiders and were eventually accepted by society, so too the Unification Church will eventually be accepted. They cite cases of extremism in the Roman

Catholic Church, claiming that the treatment of their members is no worse, and that there are Catholic parents who are unhappy at their children's decision to join the cloistered nuns' or monks' orders just as parents of Unification Church members are unhappy that their children have renounced the world to dedicate themselves to a new life.

Characteristics of the Cults

All religions have at some point in their histories been guilty of excesses. Extremism, fanaticism, and irrationality are found in all religions and, one can argue, are perhaps an essential component of all religious or mystical experiences. However, these new religious cults are *not* like the Roman Catholic Church, the Mormon Church, or other past "new religious movements." The contemporary cults exhibit characteristics that set them apart from past religious cults and from established religions. These fundamental differences make them different in kind as well as degree, and make them a unique phenomenon.

What are these characteristics? (One must remember that the following characteristics are generalizations and do not apply equally to all of the groups.)

1. Members swear total allegiance to an all-powerful leader whom they may believe to be a Messiah. The leader determines the rules for daily life and proclaims doctrines or "Truths," but generally the leader and his or her "inner circle" are exempt from the rules or prohibitions. These rules, doctrines, or "Truths" cannot be questioned. The leader's word is the absolute and final authority.

2. Rational thought is discouraged or forbidden. The groups are anti-intellectual, placing all emphasis on intuition or emotional experience. "Knowledge" is redefined as those ideas or experiences dispensed by the group or its leader. One can only attain knowledge by joining the group and submitting to its doctrine. One cannot question this "knowledge."

If the follower shows signs of doubting he is made to feel

that the fault lies within himself, not with the ideas, and he feels intensely guilty about this doubt. Says Rabbi Zalman Schacter, Professor of Religion and Jewish Mysticism at Temple University, "Any group which equates doubt with guilt is a cult."

3. The cult's recruitment techniques are often deceptive. The potential follower may not be told what he is getting into and what will be required of him. The Unification Church often does not mention its name or that of Reverend Moon for perhaps several weeks. By then the person is well indoctrinated into the movement. Most cult members probably would not join if they knew ahead of time what was involved. Says Jeannie Mills, who with her husband and five children spent six years in the People's Temple, "Your first encounter with a cult group is going to be a very pleasant experience . . . How many people would join a church if the leader stood up in front of them and said, 'You'll never have sex anymore, you're not going to have enough food to satisfy your needs, you're going to sleep four to six hours a night, and you're going to have to be cut off entirely from all your family ties?'"

4. The cult weakens the follower psychologically and makes him believe that his problems can only be solved by the group. The cult undermines all of the follower's past psychological support systems; all help from other therapy methods, psychologists or psychiatrists, religious beliefs, or parents and friends is discredited and may actually be forbidden. Psychological problems as well as intellectual doubts are soothed away by denying the reality of the conflicting feelings, by keeping the adherent so busy and constantly on the move that he has no time to think about them, and by assurances that faithful following of the cult's teachings will in time assuage them. The cult follower may reach a plateau of inner calm and appear to be free from anxiety. But this placidity may be only a mask for unresolved psychological turmoil which still presents a grave danger to the adherent.

The cult may make the follower feel helpless and dependent on the group by forcing him into childlike submission. Former

Unification Church member Christopher Edwards relates in his book *Crazy for God* how childlike he felt during a confusing game played during his recruitment:

> During the entire game our team chanted loudly, "Bomb with Love," "Blast with Love," as the soft, round balls volleyed back and forth. Again I felt lost and confused, angry, remote and helpless, for the game had started without an explanation of the rules.

He describes how he surrendered himself to the comfortable feeling of being a small child again:

> "Give in, Chris," urged a voice within me. "Just be a child and obey. It's fun. It's trusting. Isn't this the innocence, the purity of love you've been searching for?"

The cults offer total, unconditional love but actually extract a constantly higher and higher price for it—total submission to the group. Explains Edwards:

> Suddenly I understood what they wanted from me. Their role was to tease me with their love, dishing it out and withdrawing it as they saw fit. My role was not to question but to be their child, dependent on them for affection. The kiddie games, the raucous singing, the silly laughter, were all part of a scenario geared to help me assume my new identity.

5. The new cults expertly manipulate guilt. The devotee believes the group has the power to "dispense existence," to determine, according to psychologist Moshe Halevi Spero, "who has the right to live or die, physically or metaphorically." Members may be forced to "confess" their inadequacies and past "sins" before the group or certain individuals. In their book *All Gods Children* journalists Carroll Stoner and Jo Anne Parke report that "counter-cult activists claim that some religious cults keep dossiers on members and their families—the more secrets the better—in order to use the material

as emotional blackmail if the members should decide to leave, and tell of cases where this has happened."

6. Cult members are isolated from the outside world, cut off from their pasts, from school, job, family, and friends as well as from information from newspapers, radio, and television. They may be prohibited from coming and going freely into the outside world, or are so psychologically weakened that they cannot cope with it. They are told that the outside world is evil, satanic, and doomed, and that salvation can come only by remaining in the group and giving up everything else.

7. The cult or its leader makes every career or life decision for the follower. The Hare Krishna group regulates every hour of activity for those members who dwell in the temples. The cults determine every aspect of the adherent's personal life, including sexual activities, diet, use of liquor, drugs and tobacco, perhaps the choice of marriage partners, and whether, when, and how to bear children. Even if one does not live within the group the cult comes to overpower all other aspects of life. Career and schooling may be abandoned and all other interests discouraged so that the cult becomes the follower's total world.

8. Some cults promise to improve society, raise money, and work to help the poor, etc., in order to attract idealistic members. However, their energies are channeled into promoting the well-being of the group rather than towards improving society. All energy and financial resources are devoted to the cult, in some cases to the benefit only of the leaders. Cults usually exist solely for the purposes of self-survival and financial growth. While all religious organizations must be concerned with such practical affairs, these considerations are not their sole *raison d'être*.

9. Cult followers often work full time for the group. They work very long hours, for little or no pay, and in demeaning circumstances and conditions. They are made to feel guilty or unworthy if they protest. If they do work outside the group, salaries are usually turned over to the cult. The lower-echelon members may live in conditions of self-denial or extreme pov-

erty while cult leaders live comfortably or even luxuriously.
10. The cults are antiwoman, antichild, and antifamily.
Women perform the most menial tasks of cooking, cleaning,
and street solicitations and are rarely elevated to high decision-making positions in the group. Birth control, abortion,
and the physical circumstances of childbirth are often regu-
lated by the group's leaders, who are usually men. The Unification Church teaches that Eve's sin of intercourse with Satan
is the root of human estrangement from God. There are
reports of sexual abuse of women in the Church of Armageddon. A fourteen-year-old was raped in the Children of
God when she disobeyed a leader. Women in the Children of
God are encouraged to use sex to recruit new members.

There are reports of child neglect and beatings. Children are
often improperly cared for and inadequately educated. They
are at times taken away from their parents and raised by
others in the group or even geographically separated from
them. Because some members have now been in a cult for
many years, the consequences of the cult experience are af-
fecting a second generation.

Family bonds must be subordinated to loyalties to the cult,
which may speak of itself as a higher family. Children and
parents may not form close relationships because this may
threaten group loyalties. Families are often deliberately
broken up, members forced to renounce spouses who do not
approve of the group or who leave it. Cult leaders may order
"marriages" with other partners even though the follower
may be legally married to another either inside or outside of
the cult.

The followers' ties with their families outside of the group
are strained if their family disapproves of the cult, and adherents may be forced to sever connections with them. Families
are often prevented by the cult from locating their member or
from talking with him or her privately. The cult may tell the
adherent that his family is satanic and warn him that it will
try to trick him into leaving the group or may try to kidnap
him.

11. Most cult members believe the world is coming to an end and they are elite members of an "elect" survival group. They believe in a Manichean dualistic conflict between Absolute Good and Absolute Evil. By joining the cult they believe they have affiliated themselves with the Good which will eventually triumph over Evil.

They shed their old identities and take on new ones in preparation for this "new age." They have a sense of rebirth, or a starting over, and so often adopt new names, new vocabulary, and new clothing in order to purify themselves for their new lives.

12. Many of these groups have the philosophy that "the ends justify the means." Since the "ends" are so important—salvation of souls, salvation of the world, triumph of Good over Evil—any means required to carry them out are permitted and even encouraged by the cult. There may be a double standard of truth, one for cult members and another for the outside world. The cult member may be encouraged to lie to outsiders. The Unification Church practices what it calls "Heavenly Deception" and the Hare Krishna "Transcendental Trickery." The Children of God believe that since the world is so corrupt they are not subject to its laws and teach their members to subvert the legal system. However, within the cult the members must be truthful to each other and to the cult leaders.

13. The cults are often shrouded in an aura of secrecy and mystery. They keep new members in the dark, promising more knowledge about the group as they become more involved in it. Some leaders are rarely, if ever, seen by the average member. The cults may hide financial information from the public.

14. There is frequently an aura of violence or potential violence. Two Unification Church recruitment centers are guarded. The Divine Light Mission premises and the Krishnas at their farm in West Virginia have their own security forces which they insist are necessary to protect the cult leaders or to protect themselves from hostile neighbors. Many

Way International members take a weapons training course. There was a large arsenal of automatic rifles, shotguns, and handguns at Jonestown. People's Temple followers were closely guarded before Congressman Ryan and members of his party were slain and many adherents took poison or were shot by Jones's security forces.

Some cult members have been involved in incidents of beatings or shootings. In May, 1979, a Swiss court sentenced the head of a Divine Light Mission at Winterhur to fourteen years in prison on charges ranging from breach of the peace to attempted murder. In August, 1979, two Unification-Church area directors were arrested and charged with shooting at the car of two former members. Christopher Edwards' parents had to hire private detectives to guard their home for several months after he was deprogrammed and had left the Unification Church. Since Edwards' book about his experiences with the Unification Church was published, he has received two death threats. Private investigator Galen Kelly was hospitalized with a concussion for a week in 1979 after, he alleges, a Unification Church member hit him on the head with a rock.

Are the New Cults Dangerous?

Observers of the religious scene are divided over the issue of what these new groups in our society mean. Some scholars see the new cults as the "cutting edge" of a healthy and growing spiritual awakening in the Western world. They maintain that the cults promote religious pluralism by ensuring freedom of choice and a variety of religious alternatives. But cult critics perceive them as wild and poisonous weeds invading religion's vineyard. They believe the new cults are actually antipluralistic because they claim to possess the one, only, and final truth. They discourage or forbid their members to discuss other ideas and alternatives and vow to triumph over other viewpoints. This attitude, critics maintain, hinders rather than promotes religious pluralism.

We believe these new religious cults are dangerous both to

society and to their followers. They are dangerous to society because they are authoritarian and antidemocratic. They demand that the individual submit to the authority of the group, surrender his intellect to unquestioned doctrine, and subsume his life to the greater good of the group. They often encourage their members to disobey or disregard society's laws in favor of the group's mores. According to Robert Boetcher, staff director for the Fraser Congressional Subcommittee on Korean American Relations which investigated the Unification Church, Reverend Sun Myung Moon's "stated goal is to rule the world by setting up a global theocracy in which separation of church and state will be abolished."

The cults are dangerous to their followers. Although there are people who have found happiness and peace of mind, purpose and meaning in their lives through cult membership, others have paid a high price. Cults can physically endanger their followers. Cult members have been weakened by poor diet, lack of sleep, overwork, insufficient clothing as well as grim living conditions. Many groups deny proper medical care to their adherents, endangering especially those who have preexisting physical problems such as diabetes. There are reports of cult members going blind or losing their limbs because they did not get medical attention in time.

Cults are psychologically dangerous as well. Many cult members and former members have suffered severe mental breakdowns. Others have experienced a more gradual erosion of their intellectual powers and trust in their reasoning- and decision-making abilities. Even if they do get out of the group —and many do not—it may take months or even years for them to regain lost intellectual powers and a sense of well-being. Some former cult members will never regain their full potentialities. Dr. John G. Clark, Jr. testified at the hearings on religious cults conducted by Senator Robert Dole in February, 1979, that some cult members

cannot remember the past or the subtle values which would become conscience. They are often deluded, hallucinating, and confused in a new highly manipulative environment, in their altered states of consciousness. Their minds are split. They are, in effect, living in a second personality modeled on the needs of the surrounding group.

Dr. Clark continues:

To me the latest casualties of these extended manipulations are nearly unbearable to contemplate. More tortured rejects are beginning to straggle home or they are being sent home because they are useless to the cults now. Some are simply chronically psychotic, while others painfully can recognize that they cannot control the content of their minds enough to work out their life problems. Others have no flow of consciousness.

Are the cults threatening to life itself? There is evidence that this may be the case. Many adherents have disappeared inside a cult and families and friends do not know whether they are dead or alive. Some people believe many die or take their lives in these groups. At least four Unification Church members have died violently in recent years. One fell from a high floor of the church's headquarters in Manhattan. Another, William Daley, placed his head on a railroad track in Westchester County, New York, and awaited an oncoming train. In 1977 Joseph Siteman was killed when he fell between two subway cars after only two hours of sleep, having sold copies of the church's newspaper *News World.* Another member selling *News World* in a deserted neighborhood at night was the victim of street murder. Two men died in 1972 after sniffing a chemical solvent during a Church of Armageddon religious ceremony. Some babies and mothers have died in childbirth because of poor medical care. How many other cult followers have died because of inadequate medical attention? We will never know, but we do know that for over nine hundred people their search for a meaningful life ended with death in the Guyana jungle.

Is another Jonestown possible? Are there other Jim Joneses, perhaps unknown to anyone now? Do these cult leaders hold such power over their followers that they can persuade them to kill themselves—and perhaps others—at their command? Many observers of the cult scene fear the answer is "yes." Psychiatrist John Clark warned in his testimony at the Dole hearings that "these cults or groups are armies of willing, superbly controlled soldiers who would not only kill their parents or themselves, but are ready to act against anyone." Rabbi Maurice Davis of White Plains, New York, a long-time cult opponent echoes Dr. Clark's fears:

The path of segregation leads to lynching every time. The path of anti-Semitism leads to Auschwitz every time. The path of the cults leads to Jonestowns and we watch it at our peril.

Chapter 2

THE MAJOR RELIGIOUS CULTS

What are the histories, beliefs, and life-styles of the major new religious cults? How wealthy are they and how do they get their money? What do former members, parents, and other cult observers say about them? What legal problems do they face?

Because of space limitations we can discuss only a few of the fifteen hundred to three thousand new religious groups which have emerged since 1965. We have included those groups that in our judgment best represent the entire cult phenomenon.

The Unification Church

No cult has attracted more public attention than the Reverend Sun Myung Moon's controversial Unification Church. Thousands of his followers in North America, Asia, and Western Europe, derisively called "Moonies," spend long hours each day soliciting funds for their "Heavenly Father." Perpetually smiling and cheerful, Unification Church members are almost permanent fixtures at many airports, city streets, and college campuses, where they sell flowers, incense, candy, and candles to support the church's announced goal of unifying the human family in "eternal happiness, completely liberated from ignorance and directed toward goodness."

Neil Albert Salonen, the president of the American branch, says, "We don't claim to be perfect, but we are people on the road to perfection." Critics, and there are many, see that "road" leading elsewhere—to a slavelike existence for members and financial enrichment of a would-be dictator.

Moon was born in Korea in 1920 and received his early religious training at a Presbyterian mission church. According to Unification Church dogma, he experienced a vision in 1936 when Jesus appeared and confessed that his own mission two thousand years earlier had failed. He urged the Korean teenager to complete the unfinished task. Soon after this vision Moon began his ministry. Sometime following 1945 (the story is not clear) he was arrested and jailed by the North Korean government because of his strong anti-Communist views. Moon escaped from prison and fled to South Korea where, in 1954, at the age of thirty-four he established the Holy Spirit Association for the Unification of World Christianity. During this period Moon wrote the lengthy *Divine Principle,* which is the basic text of his movement. The Unification Church (the shortened name of his organization) grew slowly until 1973 when he came to the United States to take personal charge of his several hundred American followers. Since then the church has grown rapidly. There are now about thirty-seven thousand members in the United States and, it claims, nearly 3 million more throughout the world.

Reverend Moon's theology is a mixture of the Christianity he learned as a child in Korea overlaid with a form of dualism (Absolute Good vs. Absolute Evil), topped off with a version of Asian sun-god worship.

For Moon, man and woman are divine creations, but neither fully reflects God's greatness. Adam and Eve were the first humans, but Eve sinned before having perfect and sinless children. Her sexual intercourse with a serpent forever polluted the human family, which must constantly atone for this original sin. According to a 1976 *Time Magazine* report, in the early days of the Unification Church "ritual sex characterized the Moon communes. Since Moon was a pure man, sex with him ('blood cleansing') was supposed to purify both body and soul, and marriages of other cultists were in fact invalid until the wives slept with Moon."* His critics claim these sexual practices and not his political views actually caused his arrest and imprisonment. Later these practices were ended and the atonement or "indemnity" is today fulfilled through marriage in which both partners are selected by Moon.

According to Unification Church theology, a person cannot fully reflect God's nature unless he marries and has sinless children and lives in a God-centered family. Like Adam and Eve, Jesus was born sinless, but he, too, "failed" in his mission since he never married and hence had no sinless children. The God-centered family, according to Moon's teachings, is one where church members are brothers and sisters and where Moon and his wife (the current Mrs. Moon is either his third or fourth wife) are worshiped as "True Parents." A "third Adam," the "Lord of the Second Advent," will come to the world in the early 1980s to unify all peoples under his leadership. The third Adam will be a Korean who was born in 1920. In public, the church leaders do not openly claim Moon to be the Messiah; they say only that he "is preparing the way, and may prove to be the Messiah." But many members do believe he is the Messiah.

Reverend Moon claims his church is part of Christianity, but because Jesus "failed," the teachings of *Divine Principle* supersede the authority of the Bible. These claims have caused controversy within Christian theological circles. In 1977, following a study by leading Roman Catholic and Protestant scholars, the Faith and Order Commission of the Na-

*"The Darker Side of Sun Moon," *Time*, June 14, 1976, p. 50.

tional Council of Churches declared that "The claims of the Unification Church to Christian identity cannot be recognized."

The American Jewish Committee has also attacked Moon's teachings. A 1976 American Jewish Committee study cites nearly one hundred thirty specific anti-Semitic statements in *Divine Principle* and called the book "a feculent breeding ground for fostering anti-Semitism. Because of his [Moon's] unrelieved hostility towards Jews and Judaism, a demonic picture emerges from the pages of his major work.* In *Divine Principle* Jews are portrayed as "faithless," a people whose spiritual

> contents are corrupt . . . Jesus' crucifixion was the result of the ignorance and disbelief of the Jewish people . . . Satan confronted Jesus, working through the Jewish people, centering on the chief priests and scribes who had fallen faithless . . . due to the Jewish's people's rebellion against him [Jesus], the physical body of Jesus was delivered into the hands of Satan as the condition for the restoration of the Jews.

In 1971 Moon declared:

> By killing one man, Jesus, the Jewish people had to suffer for 2,000 years. Countless numbers of people have been slaughtered. During World War II, six million people were slaughtered to cleanse all the sins of the Jewish people from the time of Jesus.

Observers criticize the Unification Church's recruitment and indoctrination methods, charging they are deceptive and that the leaders employ a scientific coercive persuasion or psychological coercion technique. A close study of the church's training manual, *Master Speaks* (a collection of Moon's speeches to his followers), and interviews with former

---

*"Jews and Judaism in Reverend Moon's *Divine Principle*" by A. James Rudin. Published by the American Jewish Committee, 165 E. 56th St., New York, N.Y. 10022.

members reveal the standard recruiting technique used to gain new converts. The story of Robert T., a composite drawn from interviews with many former Unification Church members, is typical.

Robert was an outstanding high-school student and he entered his first year of college with a keen interest in philosophy and the social sciences. During his first month of college, an attractive young woman approached him on the campus and invited him to a free meal with "some of my friends" at a nearby house. When Robert arrived, he realized he was the only dinner guest present among the seven or eight other young people. The group called itself the Collegiate Association for the Research of Principle (CARP is one of the nearly seventy Unification Church front groups). Robert remembers that his dinner companions discussed the "sad and sinful condition" of the world, the need to improve society, and other moral and philosophical questions.

During the dinner his name was continually mentioned by his hosts: "Oh Robert, you're only a freshman but you know so much" . . . "Robert, could you repeat what you just said? It was so interesting!" Later that evening he attended a lecture which he found "uninspiring," but he thoroughly enjoyed the "ego stroking," and Robert was also intrigued by the group's multiethnic and multiracial makeup. At the end of the evening, one of the group's leaders took Robert aside and said, "We really loved meeting you. You fit right in and you seem so interested in our ideas. Some of the CARP members are going on a weekend retreat. Would you like to join us? It's free." Robert agreed and a few days later arrived by bus at a beautiful country estate near Tarrytown, New York.

The three-day retreat began on Friday night with the group singing such songs as "You Are My Sunshine" and "When the Red, Red Robin Comes Bob, Bob, Bobbin' Along." No drugs, sex, smoking, or alcohol were permitted, and there was no contact with the outside world through television, radio, newspapers, or telephones. Robert found himself surrounded by many overly friendly "spiritual partners." These hosts and hostesses hovered around him the entire weekend. The food was plentiful, although high in carbohydrates and low in protein. The lectures lasted from three to four hours, with no questions permitted. They were given by older men and women who appeared to possess some higher truths. The lectures described the evil forces at work among nations and the sinfulness and spiritual emptiness of individuals. The exhausting and tedious lectures were interrupted only by group singing and highly physical volleyball games.

Robert slept in a dormitory with other young men. He was never allowed to be alone; a smiling host accompanied him even when he went to the bathroom. Each night Robert and the other guests were asked to write down their innermost thoughts. The leaders collected the papers and read them at night while the recruits slept. The leaders used this information the following day by making personal references in their conversations to make the recruits think that they spontaneously had understood them.

The rest of the weekend was filled with more lectures, games, and songs. Every time Robert or anyone else tried to ask questions they were told to wait, that everything would be answered in due time. By Sunday night Robert had become so confused and bewildered that he wrote that his mind was "blown away," and later that night decided to drop out of college, quit his part-time job, and become part of the "Family." After the weekend was over he attended a seven-day workshop, a twenty-one day session, and then a six-week training period. In looking back, Robert recalls that the true identity of the group was not revealed until weeks after he was indoctrinated into the "Family." The name of Sun Myung Moon was never mentioned until the end of the six-week session when new members were taken to the top of a mountain where they held hands and prayed together. For weeks the initiates had been told that something special would soon happen to them. Finally, in a climactic ceremony the leaders revealed that Moon was their "True Parent," the one who would unify the world. Robert joyously surrendered to Moon, became an ardent disciple, a "Moonie."

Robert T. was provided with food and shelter by the church while he raised funds on the streets seven days a week for eighteen hours a day. While fund raising he ate only junk food and the food at the center where he lived was low in protein and high in starch and carbohydrates. He lost contact with his family and friends in the outside world. There was no physical or sexual contact with women in the group. All marriages were arranged by the church. In some cases partners did not even know each other beforehand. In May, 1979, Moon matched up over seven hundred couples to be married in a mass wedding sometime in 1981. The church teaches that all persons, both living and dead, must be sexually matched in order to achieve spiritual salvation. Neil Salonen told a group of Evangelical Christian leaders in 1979 that Jesus has been matched with a young woman now living in Korea. Salonen believes that several drops of Reverend Moon's blood were added to the wine used at the church's first engagement ceremony in 1960. The original wine has been preserved for use in future ceremonies, and the diluted wine still contains Moon's blood.

What happened to Robert T. has happened to thousands of other Unification-Church recruits. Over and over again, the nearly identical pattern of recruitment is reported. Critics assert these similarities are no accident. Steve Hassan, a former Unification-Church high official who was a national leader of CARP, believes the marathon lectures are a form of hypnosis. "Three forces were at work in the lectures," Steve explains:

> repetition, monotony, and rhythm. These are the same factors present in hypnosis, I found out later. And the recruitment period was constantly filled with suggestions that something wonderful was about to happen. They got everybody primed for it. The Unification leaders reinterpreted the past, manipulated

the present, and appeared to be in possession of the future. They seemed to know what the future would be like, and it was up to the recruit whether or not to join in with the vision.

Philip Cushman, who operates the West Coast Jewish Training Project in San Francisco and counsels former cult members and their families, believes the church's recruitment methods and techniques are improving and becoming stronger. Cushman, who will not "snatch" anyone from a cult for rehabilitation, says it is getting more and more difficult to persuade Unification Church members to come out of the group's premises to talk to their families or to deprogrammers. "Recently it's been harder," he says, "the Moonies obviously have a new and highly effective technique for keeping them from seeing their families or friends at the last minute."

Like Robert T., Steve Hassan was attracted by the church's sense of being a family. Yet one midnight in the spring of 1976 the "Family" deserted Steve when he rammed his car into the back of a truck on the Baltimore Beltway after seventy-two continuous hours of fund raising. Following the accident he was taken to a hospital for an operation where he faced the possible amputation of his legs. Steve fully expected the "Family" to assist him in his recovery, but instead the Unification Church leaders contacted Steve's sister and parents and informed them of the accident. They rushed to take care of him. His legs were saved and during the long period of recuperation he was deprogrammed and left the church.

Steve is bitter when he remembers how quickly the church deserted him after his automobile accident. "I deeply believed the group was a loving family that cared about its members. As soon as I was seriously injured and could no longer collect funds or recruit, the Family called my satanic real family. The Moonies couldn't get rid of me fast enough!"

The church's seemingly unfeeling behavior towards Steve is explained in one of its training manuals. The church follower is told precisely what to do when a friend is wounded or injured in the "fight against Satan":

> If you leave him [the friend], he will die. If you help him, he won't die for now, but you will lose the battle. Not because you don't love your brother, but because you do love him, you must leave him and attack the enemy and subjugate the enemy and afterwards come back and maybe already he is dead. Then with tears, we embrace the dead body of our friend.*

Allen Tate Wood, Christopher Edwards, and many other former Unification Church members can recount similar stories of abuse and humiliation. Wood charges that the church exploits its members by its marathonlike fundraising activies. Wood, who headed the church in Maryland and was the "Commander of the One World Crusade" prior to his deprogramming, relates:

> I attended all the National Directors' conferences. I heard Moon speak ten hours a day. It was like being in a business meeting with a body count; how many businesses opened, how many new members, how much money coming in, who was being influenced politically? There was not one iota of emotion felt.

In 1979 Wood publicly claimed that the church took in anywhere from $109 million to $219 million annually by direct street solicitations. He said the church has two thousand workers on the streets seven a days a week, each collecting between $150 and $300 per day. In 1979 former church member Ellen Lloyd told an Illinois state legislative investigating committee that she sent nearly $10,000 each week to the personal New York bank account of Reverend Moon. She declared that Moon may also have received up to ten times that amount each week from other church-related

---

*Sudo, Ken. "Practical Aspects of Training: How to be a Good Leader," (Unification Church Training Manual, May, 1975), p. 375.

groups in Illinois. Critics charge that the Unification Church practices "Heavenly Deception" (a church term) upon the public and that this enables them to raise such large amounts of money. The group "raises money in Idaho and says it's for a charitable purpose, but sends it to New York to invest in a restaurant," Allen Tate Wood explains.

Following Wood's revelation that the church raises from $109 to $219 million annually, Unification Church officials admitted that the group collected about $20 million in 1978, 90 percent from street solicitations. This is a dramatic increase over the $8 million it claimed to have raised in 1975. Although neither the $219 million figure Wood gives nor the $20 million the church claims can be verified, but it is clear the Unification Church is a multimillion-dollar-a-year operation in the United States alone.

Moon has used these millions to acquire vast real-estate holdings as well as many businesses, most nontaxable because of the organization's status as a religious group. In 1975 and 1976 the church purchased such major New York City properties as the New Yorker Hotel, the Columbia Club, Manhattan Center, the old Tiffany's building on Fifth Avenue, and the former Loft's candy factory in Queens. Other purchases include 410 acres in Westchester County, New York (including Reverend Moon's 22-acre Tarrytown residence formerly owned by the Samuel Bronfman family), a 235-acre Hudson River estate in Tarrytown, New York, that houses the church's seminary, two camps in California used for recruitment and indoctrination, the former Eben Jordan mansion on Boston's Beacon Street, houses in Berkeley, California, Marblehead, Massachusetts, New York City, and centers in many other American cities. In 1978 the church purchased the Chisleheart Convent in Kent, England, from the Roman Catholic Sisters of Mercy. The nuns did not learn the true identity of the buyer until after the sale and were so distressed that they issued a public statement saying "they would not have agreed to the sale" had they known their convent would become a Unification-Church center. In 1979, the church bought at public auction a 100-acre Roman Catholic retreat center in Chappaqua, New York.

Bob Sullivan, Neil Salonen's assistant, acknowledges that the church "eventually wants to shift the emphasis from fund raising and put the emphasis on business." The Unification Church owns many businesses in Korea, including the highly controversial Tong II armaments manufacturing factory near Seoul. It also owns a printing company in San Francisco, a restaurant in Manhattan, and holds the Ginseng Tea monopoly in the United States. Using the name International Oceanic Enterprises, the church operates fish-processing plants in Virginia, California, and Alaska, tuna- and lobster-fishing operations in Massachusetts, and a boat-building enterprise in Alabama. The Security and Exchange Commission charges that the Unification Church sought to achieve secret control of Diplomat National Bank in Washington, D.C. The church owns the daily New York City newspaper, *News World*. In 1977 a *Washington Post* reporter charged that *News World* had printed unauthorized advertisements. The paper's editorial policy has consistently supported the repressive South-Korean government and the minority white regimes in southern Africa. It has turned its strongest journalistic guns on former Representative Donald Fraser, its leading congressional critic. In the fall of 1979 the Unification Church invested from $18 to 35 million in a movie about the Korean War called INCHON. The movie's producer, Mitsuharu Ishii, is head of the Japanese division of Tong II industry, a Unification Church-owned defense contractor, and is a top financial adviser to Reverend Moon.

Wherever the Unification Church has purchased property or established businesses, the affected communities have often sought to combat the group by legal means. In Westchester County the Tarrytown Board of Trustees unanimously approved a zoning ordinance that prevented the church from building a university complex there. Senator Lowell Weicker of Connecticut has called for an investigation of the church's fishing interests based on charges that Unification Church fishing enterprises have an unfair advantage over other American fisheries. Business competitors contend that over half of the church's fishery employees are church members who turn over their earnings to the group or who are paid substandard wages. Thus, the church fisheries can sell their catches for less money. In 1978 the thirteen-member New York State Board of Regents unanimously rejected the application of the Unification Seminary in Barrytown to become a degree-granting institution. The Board refused the accreditation because it claimed the seminary did not meet minimum academic standards, had a questionable financial structure, and had made certain deceptive claims. A local citizens' group in Chappaqua, New York, is attempting legally to prevent the church from using the former Roman Catholic retreat center it recently purchased as Unification Church recruitment headquarters.

The church's political goals and programs are under close scrutiny. At the core of Moon's teaching is an unrelenting, hard-line anti-Communism. It views countries such as North Korea and the Soviet Union as satanic powers, while the United States and South Korea are "Heavenly" states committed to truth and Godliness. In one of its many legal battles to retain tax-exempt status for its properties the Unification Church defended its anti-Communist activities by saying they are part of its religious beliefs. As one Unification Church official explained, "Our approach is to have a political effect caused by a religious concern."

Moon has also been active in American politics. He strongly supported Richard Nixon's presidency. In November, 1973, during calls for Nixon's impeachment, Moon asserted in a *New York Times* advertisement: "At this moment in history God has chosen Richard Nixon to be President of the United States of America. Therefore, God has the power and authority to dismiss him." Moon called the President "archangel Nixon," and in late January, 1974, Unification Church members held a parade and rally in Lafayette Square where they met with the President's daughter and son-in-law, Tricia and

Edward Cox. On the morning following the rally, Moon met privately with Nixon in the White House.

Critics also charge Moon sent hundreds of his female followers to Capitol Hill in 1975 and 1976 to serve as Congressional aides and secretaries. In a 1979 *Playboy* article deprogrammer Ted Patrick claimed young Unification Church women were ordered "to approach every congressman and senator and lure him" to a plush hotel suite. "Once they did, they were served good food, and there was dancing and anything else that followed . . . there were beautiful American, Korean, and Japanese girls. It was their job to get them into bed." According to Patrick the unsuspecting legislators would then get a telephone call a few days later saying a tape had been made of their recent hotel visit. Patrick believes this accounts for the inability of Congress to probe the cults thoroughly. Unification Church officials have denied Patrick's allegations.

Church critics contend that a working arrangement was developed in the 1960s between the South Korean government of the late President Park Chung Hee and Moon for the purpose of "influencing United States foreign policy" toward Korea. This close linkage was revealed in November, 1978, by the United States House Subcommittee on International Organizations headed by former Representative Donald Fraser of Minnesota. The report called for a federal interagency task force to investigate the apparent illegal activities of the Unification Church and its many related operations. The Fraser Subcommittee cited violations of United States tax, immigration, banking, currency, and foreign registration laws by the Unification Church. The 447-page report charged that the

Moon organization promoted the interests of the Republic of Korea Government . . . attempted to obtain permission from an American corporation to export M-16 rifles manufactured in Korea . . . The Unification Church, essentially one international organization, attempts to achieve goals outlined by Sun Myung

Moon, who has substantial control over the economic, political, and spiritual activities . . . Among the goals is the establishment of a worldwide government in which the separation of church and state would be abolished and which would be governed over by Moon and his followers.*

The Fraser report listed many other Unification Church political activities "undertaken to benefit the Republic of Korea . . . to create political influence for itself and the Republic of Korea Government . . . related to the organization's overall goals of gaining temporal power." Three months after the report was issued, the Unification Church issued a 221-page denial of the charges.

But Moon's speeches to his followers clearly reveal his quest for political power and the ways he would use such power. In March, 1974, Moon said:

Some day in the near future, when I walk into the Congressman's or the Senator's offices without notice or appointment, the aides will jump out of their seats and go to get their Senator or Congressman, saying he must see Reverend Moon. The time will come, without my seeking it, that my words will almost serve as law. If I ask a certain thing, it will be done. If I don't want something, it will not be done. If I recommend a certain Ambassador for a certain country, and then visit that country . . . he will greet me with the red carpet treatment.**

Moon told his followers "if and when we have a nation of our own restored to God's side, how fast will our mission be realized? By that time we can stir up the whole world . . . I am a thinker, I am your brain." Speaking of himself in the third person, Moon has declared that "if he finds it impossible to do his

*Final Report, "Investigation of Korean-American Relations", Subcommittee on International Organizations of the United States House of Representatives International Relations Committee, October 31, 1978. United States Government Printing Office, Washington, D.C.

**Master Speaks (Unification Church, on the occasion of Parent's Day, March 24, 1974), p. 9

work in America, he will go to Germany . . . Germans are trained in totalism, so it will be easier to work on his mission there."

Is there a potential for violence in the Unification Church? Several former church members, including Shelly Turner, Virginia Mabry, and Philip Kashian report that Moon encourages suicide among his followers. Ms. Mabry recounts a December, 1976, lecture in San Francisco where the members were told to make their suicide appear as murder if they had no chance to escape a deprogrammer. "The best thing," she said, "would be to throw ourselves in front of the deprogrammer's car, because he would be charged with murder. Second, depending on how much time we have, we were told to slice either our wrist or our jugular vein." In one of his speeches that appear in *Master Speaks,* Moon asks his followers: "Have you ever thought you may die for the Unification Church? . . . We are the elite of heavenly soldiers and you must be determined to win the battle . . . with you as a bullet, whatever you pierce through will be either killed or remade." A basic training manual instructs Unification Church members, "Therefore, don't have any consciousness of existence—just serve."

The International Society for Krishna Consciousness

On August 3, 1976, Merylee Kreshower, now known by the Indian name of Murti Vanya, was taken by her mother, Edyth, to a motel room where Galen Kelly, a private investigator, attempted to deprogram her from the Hare Krishna group.

Miss Kreshower filed kidnaping charges against her mother and Kelly. But after an extensive hearing during which the ideas and practices of the Hare Krishna were probed, two New York Krishna leaders, Angus Murphy and Harold Conley, were indicted and charged with unlawful imprisonment and use of mind control of Merylee Kreshower and another Hare Krishna member who had been called into the case as a material witness, Eddie Shapiro. They were also charged with grand larceny for attempting to extort $20,000 from Eddie's father, prominent Boston physician Eli Shapiro, who was attempting to get his diabetic son out of the group.

In March, 1977, Queens Supreme Court Criminal Division Judge John J. Leahy dismissed all charges against the Hare Krishna officials, ruling that no crime had been committed and that the real issue was one of freedom of choice of religion. He judged the Hare Krishna movement, officially known as ISKCON (International Society for Krishna Consciousness) to be a "bona fide religion" and said that the two followers had a right to pursue their chosen life. The celebrated case was declared a great legal and moral victory for the Hare Krishna movement in its first legal test. Both Merylee Kreshower and Eddie Shapiro returned to Hare Krishna. They are still there.

Parents of young people like Merylee and Eddie cannot understand why their children want to belong to this very strict group. Every aspect of their daily lives is tightly prescribed and controlled by a rigid time schedule. Full-time adherents who live in Hare Krishna temples arise at 3:45 A.M. for four hours of meditation and chanting before their strenuous day's work begins. The devotional clothing they must wear is a symbol of their renunciation of material pleasures and commitment to the spiritual life. The women wear Indian saris, the men wear robes called "dhotis," white for the married and saffron for the celibate unmarried. Leather shoes are forbidden. The men's heads are shaved except for a top knot or braid, the "shika," by which, it is said, Lord Krishna can pull them into heaven.

Devotees must follow strict Hindu dietary laws. They can eat no meat, eggs, or fish because the killing of animals is forbidden; they can drink no coffee, tea, or colas, and they cannot smoke or use drugs. They eat twice a day and always first offer the food as a sacrifice to the god Krishna. Meals consist primarily of vegetables, rice, fruit, cream of wheat, sweet milk, a mixture of yogurt, milk and fruit juices called nectar, and raw gingerroot. Dried bean mush and raw chick peas are the primary sources of protein. The food is generally the same every day except for special feasts, because the Krishnas believe that if the tongue is allowed a taste of enjoyment desire for other enjoyments will follow.

The most important activity of the full-time Hare Krishna member is chanting. They must repeat at least sixteen times a day, while fingering prayer beads, the famous chant, "Hare Krishna, Hare Krishna, Krishna Krishna, Hare Hare, Hare Rama, Hare Rama, Rama Rama, Hare Hare." This is a recital of names for and praises of the god Krishna, and it may be repeated hundreds and even thousands of times a day.

About one half of full-time Krishnas are married. The marriages are arranged by the group, and no divorce is allowed. The couple usually do not live together. They sleep in sexually segregated dormitories and might even work in separate cities. Children do not go to public schools; they are sent away to Krishna boarding schools called "gurukalas" where they study Hindu scriptures and chanting. The Hare Krishna educators particularly eschew "Darwin and Dewey"—the teaching of evolution and modern, progressive education.

Sexual activity outside of marriage is forbidden. Within marriage sex is a duty. It is for procreation only, a "necessary evil," and not for sensual enjoyment. Intercourse takes place only one day a month, when the woman is most fertile, after several hours of chanting has cleansed the mind. All other physical contact, even kissing, between husband and wife is forbidden. There is no physical contact between unmarried men and women, who are not allowed to be alone together. All activities at the centers are segregated.

The woman must submit herself with humility to her husband, as women play a subservient role to all the men in the group. The men perform the temple rituals because, according to Laxmi Nrshimha, the president of the Hare Krishna temple in Manhattan, they are better equipped spiritually. Women are too tied to the material world. "The form of a woman," explains Nrshimha, the former Lawrence Pugliesi, "is more prone to sex life, more prone to sense gratification. It's harder for them to control their drives and they often need to get married." Men organize and direct the temple administration while women prepare the food, clean the temples, and bathe and dress the statues of the gods, all under the men's supervision. Women are forbidden to look a man in the eye and must instead look at his feet. The men eat first; Susan Murphy reports that in her Boston temple the women were fed "like dogs" with scraps from the table after the men had finished eating. In an interview in *Back to Godhead,* the Hare Krishna magazine, the founder, His Divine Grace A. C. Bhaktivedanta Swami Prabhupada, explains that women can never be equal to men because of their child-bearing functions and their lower mentality and that if women do not subordinate themselves to men, they become burdens to society. According to a former Krishna, the leader of the Boston temple preaches that women's brains weigh thirty-two ounces while men's brains weigh sixty-four ounces.

Still, many devotees appear to be very happy. Some observers and parents who visit their children in the temples comment on the contentment and joy they appear to have found. The founder believes his movement provides satisfaction because it is a practical system for reaching God, not a useless speculative philosophy.

The Indian holy man, now considered by his followers to be an incarnation of the god Krishna, came to New York in 1965 with fifty rupees, then worth about $6.00, in his pocket. In 1966 he set up a storefront mission on New York's lower East Side, sermonized in Greenwich Village parks, and offered free vegetarian meals, attracting primarily "hippies" and drug addicts. With the help of other Indian gurus in the United States and attention from the media, Prabhupada's ISKCON grew and widened its appeal. Even his death in November, 1977, did not halt the spread of this Americanized Hindu movement.

According to Hare Krishna officials there are now about ten to twelve thousand initiated full-time members in the United States, living in forty temples. They estimate there are tens of thousands of additional "lay" or "congregational" members who live and work outside of the group and attend religious and social events in the temples. There are over one hundred Krishna centers in Africa, Asia, Europe, Israel, Latin America, Canada, Australia, and New Zealand. One ISKCON leader says they plan to expand to China.

They own two dozen large urban properties, including a fourteen-story temple and residence on West 55th Street in Manhattan, reported to have cost $1 million. They are building a large solar energy pyramid-style house in Los Angeles' Topango Canyon, and own eleven other buildings within a four-block area of Los Angeles which house the "New Dwarka" community of 400 Krishnas.

They own and operate farms in India, France, England, Italy, Brazil, Australia, and New Zealand. There are six farms in the United States, all larger than one hundred acres, located in Mississippi, Florida, Pennsylvania, West Virginia, California, and Tennessee. They grow vegetables and raise cattle for milk on the largest, 1,500 acres, near Moundsville, West Virginia. Called "New Vrindaban," it is a haven for traveling Krishnas.

In January, 1978, the group dedicated a new $2 million temple complex in a suburb of Bombay, India. In the fall of 1979 construction was finished on an elaborate temple on fifty acres of the West Virginia property. It is called Prabhupada Palace in memory of their founder. Kirtanananda Swami, Prabhupada's American-born successor and about three hundred other Krishnas occupy it. The building is crowned by a twenty-four-carat gold leaf dome, has terraces, moats, and gardens and is decorated with two hundred tons of marble from forty countries, crystal chandeliers, stained-glass peacocks, and teakwood doors. The Krishnas built the temple themselves over a period of ten years and so claim it cost only about $500,000. They plan to build six more temples, a restaurant, formal gardens, a hotel, greenhouses, and a school on the site.

They maintain their property is largely financed by contributions from sympathetic Indians in California. They have received help also from former Beatle George Harrison, who gave $100,000 towards the Prabhupada Palace and donated a 23-acre estate sixteen miles from London. Krishna devotee Alfred Ford, Henry Ford's great-grandson, pays for the leases on their warehouses in California, is financing a Hare Krishna museum in Detroit, and lent the temple in Detroit money to buy the former Fisher mansion there. Another Krishna, Lisa Reuther, daughter of the late Walter Reuther, also donated her inheritance to make the purchase possible.

The movement earns about 70 percent of its income from magazine and book sales. *Newsweek* estimates this literature earns $20 million a year. Prabhupada wrote fifty-two books which have sold more than 65 million copies. The Hare Krishna Publishing Trust is now compiling additional books from his lectures and letters. The devotees sell these publications when they solicit on street corners, in parks, and in airports. From this soliciting, which they consider a religious duty called "Sankirtan," each devotee can earn $100 a day. Sales and contributions reap an estimated $7 million a year.

They have other flourishing business enterprises. They produce and market "Spiritual Sky Incense," operate restaurants in Los Angeles, London, Iran, Honolulu, Amsterdam, and New York, sell Hare Krishna cookbooks, and in 1978 launched a food-catering service in Los Angeles.

The Krishnas object to being called a "new religious movement" since they claim descent from four thousand-year-old Hinduism. They explain that their movement is a continuation of a reformation instigated by a sixteenth-century holy man who offered the poor a means of salvation through love of Krishna expressed by singing, dancing, and chanting. Prabhupada distinguished himself from other gurus such as Transcendental Meditation's Maharishi Mahesh Yogi and Maharaj Ji of the Divine Light Mission. He says they are "rascals" because they simply sell their mantras and make no demands on their followers.

Krishnas do not want their movement classified as a religious "cult" and cite differences between ISKCON and other groups. Their leaders do not live in luxury and are not immoral. They do not, they claim, require members to cut ties with their families and friends, and contend that over half of the parents approve of the group. Followers can decide for themselves how much of their time they want to devote—they can be "lay" rather than full-time members. They claim their recruiting techniques are not deceptive, that their fund raisers always identify themselves, and that the followers are free to leave the group. They quote testimony from parents and mental-health "experts" that their chanting techniques do not harm the mind, and say that they encourage intellectual development through the study of Sanskrit and Hindu scripture. Unlike the cults, their organization, they maintain, is not authoritarian. A twenty-four-member international board governs democratically. The board chooses eleven senior disciples or "spiritual masters" whose authority stems from Hindu scripture and who can be removed if they abuse it.

But critics contend that ISKCON does have many characteristics of the other cults. They argue that many members have been forcibly cut off from their families, sometimes moved around from temple to temple throughout the world so that their parents cannot find them. Some parents of young children who were taken into the group by their estranged spouses or who were born there accuse the Krishnas of hiding them. Jerry Yanoff of Chicago discovered his missing twelve-year-old son, David, in a Los Angeles temple. "I was attacked by devotees and David was torn screaming from my arms," Yanoff relates. After a long campaign he finally recovered David from the group. In April, 1979, a former Krishna leader, Cheryl Wheeler, brought suit to obtain custody of her eight-year-old son Devin, whom she had to leave behind when she left the group. She claims that every time she tries to get Devin the Krishnas give a different excuse for not being able to find him.

Former members charge that their health deteriorated for lack of proper nutrition and medical care. Susan Murphy told a Massachusetts legislative committee that ISKCON is "antihuman": "After years of chanting and indoctrination," she testified, "of ill health, bad diet, and vermin-infested living conditions, years of brainwashing and being forced to beg on the street, I finally realized that Krishna had turned me and the other women into slaves." She revealed that it is not always easy to leave the group. Dissenters are "encouraged to commit suicide, or told that Krishna will harm them."

Critics claim ISKCON discourages rational thought. One of its basic premises is that reason keeps one from finding God; the Hare Krishna prohibition against gambling forbids all forms of "mental speculation," critics say. Devotees must chant constantly. *Snapping* authors Flo Conway and Jim Siegelman contend this constant chanting reinforces the mental state that may have been altered by the powerful mystical experiences induced by elaborate temple ceremonies. Krishnas are especially encouraged to chant when they begin to doubt or question ISKCON beliefs or their commitment to them. Chanting soothes the mental conflict, explain Conway and Siegelman, because one concentrates on the sounds and repetition of the words rather than on the anxious thoughts. When done over a long period of time, chanting may, according to a former ISKCON high official who does not publicly identify himself "lead to complete dissolution of the mind." This official claims there are many mental "vegetables," "basket cases" in the temples and that Hare Krishna's worst mental casualties may be hidden away from the world in their large West Virginia farm. "There are people cracking all the time," he told Conway and Siegelman. "Either they become vegetables or crack violently."

But it is ISKCON's solicitation techniques that evoke the most widespread criticism. Krishnas do not always identify themselves when soliciting, as they claim. Some people approached for money contend the devotees told them they were collecting for other causes such as a Roman Catholic mission, the Muscular Dystrophy Foundation, or the Christian Science Church. They sometimes solicit in street clothing and so are not readily identifiable. Six members were taken into custody in Chicago in December, 1977, because they were fund raising in the Loop in Santa-Claus suits.

Critics claim ISKCON members harass exhausted travelers at international airports, often preying on foreigners who do not understand English. Some travelers are verbally and even physically assaulted if they do not donate. In January, 1979, Western Airlines mechanic Paul Marks claimed a Krishna attacked him with what "appeared to be brass knuckles" during an argument in the Los Angeles airport. Other airport personnel there say the Hare Krishnas threatened to beat or kill them when they advised passengers of their real identity.

Some Krishna devotees use more subtle techniques in their fund raising. They concentrate on the potential donor's particular interests, and joke and smile. Sometimes they plead to keep the change from a large bill or simply refuse to give change. The Krishnas term such devices "Transcendental Trickery." Explained one Krishna to an interviewer on a July, 1979, "Prime Time Sunday" television program, "trickery is all right if we're doing it for God." They maintain that in forcing people to donate, they are saving their souls by preventing them from spending the money on material goods. Since the world is doomed, it is their duty to save as many souls as quickly as possible in this way.

Former Krishna Susan Murphy and her mother sued the Boston group for $2.5 million in 1977, charging it with false imprisonment, violations of state child labor laws (Susan was only thirteen when she joined), breach of contract, deceit, fraud, infliction of mental distress, destruction of the Murphy family, invasion of privacy, seduction of a minor (she claims that she was forced to live with a male Krishna), and assault and battery. Other legal battles have centered around attempts to curb Hare Krishna solicitation efforts. In the past, courts upheld their right to solicit in public parks, on streets, and in airports. But in September, 1979, Superior Court Judge Robert L. Weil severely restricted their soliciting practices at the Los Angeles International Airport. Managers of about twenty other airports are attempting to limit Krishna solicitations to certain areas within the terminals. At the Atlanta airport Krishnas have been restricted to soliciting money within designated booths located in the main lobby and concourse area, although they may pass out literature outside of the booths.

Conflicts between the Hare Krishna and the public are not confined to the law courts. Since 1973, Krishnas at the farm in Moundsville, West Virginia, have been stockpiling large numbers of weapons, including M-14 semiautomatic rifles and handguns and thousands of rounds of ammunition. The Krishnas claim the weapons are for self-defense to protect themselves from their violent neighbors. There have been sporadic shooting incidents between the Hare Krishna members and locals—the Krishnas speak of the conflict as a battle between the "demons" and the "devotees"—since June 1973. However, the Moundsville townspeople seem to be adjusting to the Krishnas and the shooting incidents have stopped. The Krishnas plan to open the newly built Prabhupada Palace temple there to the public as a "spiritual theme park" called "Krishnaland" so outsiders can see their home firsthand and better understand their way of life.

The Way International

"Open the doors to a powerful and victorious life!" Such is the invitation extended by Dr. Victor Paul Wierwille to enroll in one of his "Power for Abundant Living" classes. A Way International brochure claims the class "establishes and maintains a positive attitude, makes life meaningful, overcomes worry and fear, increases prosperity, explains Bible contradictions, develops more harmony in the home, enables you to separate truth from error, disciplines the mind by believing, teaches how to pray effectually, and maintains health."

Now in his early sixties, the dynamic and charismatic Wierwille studied at the University of Chicago and Princeton

Theological Seminary to become an Evangelical and Reformed Church clergyman. From his first "Abundant Living" seminars in October, 1953, emerged The Way International, now centered on a 147-acre former farm in New Knoxville, Ohio. Wierwille describes his organization as a nondenominational, nonsectarian Bible research program.

About two hundred Way followers live and study at the New Knoxville center. They claim twenty to one hundred thousand additional members throughout the United States and in fifty-one other countries. They compare their steady growth to that of a tree from a small seed and speak of their members as leaves, local fellowship houses as twigs, area-wide fellowship centers as branches, the state organization as limbs, the national organization in New Knoxville as the trunk, and the Board of Directors, headed by Wierwille, as the root of the tree.

Way followers are predominently in their late teens or early twenties, but they enroll anyone twelve years of age or older in their Bible classes and have some older members, who are often parents of Way followers. The members are for the most part affluent and future- and success-oriented.

Observers estimate The Way's income is about $1 million per year. They have $20 million in property holdings, including the entire campus of Emporia College in Kansas which they renovated for $2 million. The Way operates a publishing house, The American Christian Press, and a recording company. It owns a $750,000 jet airplane and two customized motorbuses used for evangelizing.

Bible classes provide The Way International's major source of income. The "Power for Abundant Living" course, fifteen three-hour sessions of films and videotapes of Wierwille's lectures, costs $100. To be trained in Way recruitment and evangelization methods one must join "The Way Corps" by paying $300 a month for training at the Emporia campus. Their goal is to enroll over 3 million in The Way Corps program by 1990. Income comes also from the sale of "Trustee Notes," bonds that pay an annual interest rate of 6 percent. All members must tithe. One Catholic priest asserts the movement receives 20 to 30 percent of its followers' incomes. Local leaders must support themselves with outside jobs while working full-time in The Way ministry.

Wierwille's unorthodox theology has upset many Christians, especially those whose children have been attracted to the group. They claim Wierwille preaches the old Christian heresy of Arianism since he rejects the doctrines of the Trinity and the divinity of Jesus. Wierwille maintains there can be no disagreement about or interpretation of Scripture, which is God-given and final—"The Word means what it says, and it says what it means"—so Way Bible students use only the King James Version and employ no "man-made" exegetical study aids. Wierwille criticizes other forms of Christianity and looks upon anyone not following The Way as "natural man," lost to salvation and "the abundant life."

Many parents of Way members object to calling the group a cult. They claim their children were not pressured into joining and are free to leave. They say they are happy and well adjusted and there is no violence in the group. Other parents and former Way members disagree. They point out that Bible classes are denied to those who cannot pay. One cannot take notes, tape lectures, or ask questions during the "Power for Abundant Living" course. They claim Wierwille promotes tensions between Way members and their families by teaching that Way followers need not answer to "natural man."

Several former Way members charge they were subjected to mind-control techniques. After strenuous morning exercising and working at his job all day, one young man had to spend many hours a night "fellowshiping" and then stay up late reading Scripture and Wierwille's books. "You are so dead tired that you can't think straight," and he says,

. . . this is when they really get heavy and start coming down on you . . . You are at the point where you are so physically and

mentally fatigued that you are going to take exactly what they
say for granted. I was a victim of mind control . . . you are so
brainwashed that anything they tell you, you are going to believe.

Former member Sharon Bell asserts The Way administers
Kool-Aid mixed with drugs and that she got only three hours
of sleep a night and lived on rice and potatoes. A cult critic,
New Jersey physician Harold Scales, reports that students at
The Way College participate in "colon-cleanse" programs in
which they combine a diet of laxatives, detoxicants, green-life
vitamin tablets, water, and juice with colonic enemas, which
could badly weaken already malnourished members. Sharon
Bell says Way members told her "it might be necessary to kill
anyone who tried to leave the group." Timothy Goodwin was
told the devil would kill him if he left. *The Ohio Magazine* reports that the two books recommended for reading at a Way
study seminar in the summer of 1979 were *The Myth of the Six
Million* and *The Hoax of the Twentieth Century*. Both books
assert that 6 million Jews were not killed by the Nazis during
World War II, that these stories are a hoax perpetrated by
"left-wing intellectuals."

Townspeople in New Knoxville are leery of The Way police
force which patrols the group's property with walkie-talkies
and handguns. The organization claims it needs its own security force because trespassers fire guns on its property and
local police can't respond fast enough to complaints. Many
people also object to the ten-hour weapons training classes in
which Way followers learn marksmanship with .22 caliber
rifles at the Emporia campus. In 1976 and 1977 more than five
hundred Way members took these courses. The Way claims
they are teaching their members hunting safety, but critics
say the group maintains armed training camps.

Deprogrammer Kurt Van Gorden hints he was threatened
by the group when he criticized it in lectures in New Knoxville
in March, 1979. He contends a .45 caliber bullet was dropped
into the collection bucket during one of the lectures, The Way

Police Force circled the home where he went afterwards, and telephone callers threatened to interrupt other speeches. Raymond and Lois Bell of Falls Church, Virginia, also claim Way members trailed them in cars, made threatening telephone calls, and broke into their home after having had their daughter, Sharon, deprogrammed from the group.

In August, 1979, a Fairfax County judge ordered The Way to stop harassing the Bells. In another legal struggle Timothy Goodwin sued the group and in an out-of-court settlement was repaid money he had donated to it. Goodwin had pledged to the group 15 percent of a $1.4 million settlement from an automobile accident which had left him a quadriplegic. He says Way members had assured him their prayers would heal him. He had also made out a will leaving all of his money to the group.

Tony and Susan Alamo Christian Foundation

"He's mine now. He will never return to you."

These are the words that Mrs. Ida Kitchener, a Flushing, New York mother, heard from Susan Alamo in 1969 after she begged Mrs. Alamo to let her son, Bob, out of her religious commune. Bob Kitchener is one of hundreds of young people —estimates range from two hundred to seven hundred fifty— in the Tony and Susan Alamo Christian Foundation, one of the surviving Jesus People movements from the 1960s.

Susan Alamo was born Edith Opal Horn over fifty years ago in Dyer, Arkansas. She was married twice, then under the name of Susan Fleetwood tried to become an actress in Hollywood. In 1964 she founded a religious organization, the Susan Lipowitz Foundation (Lipowitz was the name of her second husband), but it failed.

Tony, in his forties, whose real name is Bernard Lazar Hoffman, was born and raised a Jew in Joplin, Missouri. He changed his name to Tony Alamo because, as he explains it, "Italians at the time were making it big as singers," and he tried to become a vocalist. He ended up instead as a successful show business promoter. In Los Angeles he was convicted of receiving and concealing stolen property and served three months in prison. In 1964 he pleaded guilty to a charge of mail fraud and received a $500 fine and one year's probation. He recounts that in 1964 the voice of God told him to give up his way of life and to preach the gospel. He did nothing about his "calling" until Susan Fleetwood, who became his third wife, converted him, and in 1969 they started their tax-exempt Tony and Susan Alamo Christian Foundation.

Their first converts were drug addicts and young vagrants who hung out on Los Angeles' Hollywood Boulevard. The Alamos first took them to their home and later by shuttle bus to the Alamo Foundation camp at Saugus, a suburb forty miles north of Los Angeles. They preached "hellfire-and-damnation" sermons to them about the God of Wrath who will soon destroy the world. According to one former Foundation member, Sandy Wenderoth, the young people were told, once they got out to the camp, that there was no way to get back to Los Angeles, and that they might as well spend the night there. They were assigned an "older Christian," a counselor who never left them alone.

Today the Alamo Foundation still owns property—a 160-acre farm—and businesses in California, but its main headquarters are in Alma, Arkansas. There they operate a large restaurant that seats 600 people and is open twenty-four hours a day, a gasoline station, a Western clothing shop, a cement company, and a construction business. The "Alamos of Nashville" clothing store in Nashville, Tennessee, sells expensive Western clothing such as thousand-dollar rhinestone suits to the wealthy country and Western singing crowd, many of whom are friends of Tony and Susan. The Alamos own a home in an exclusive section of Nashville. The Foundation reportedly earns over $1 million per year from its business operations, property, and donations.

The teenagers and young adults work long hours—as much as twelve hours a day, some critics claim—for little or no pay in the Alamo-owned businesses. They do not work or live outside of the group and have minimal contact with outsiders. All basic physical needs are met by the commune. Men and women live separately, are never allowed to be alone together, and speak to each other only at mealtimes. Tony and Susan approve all marriages, and before the marriage ceremony the couple is separated for ninety days of prayer and fasting. A hierarchical group of "elders" or "overseers" controls the group with strict discipline, allowing no drugs, drinking, or dancing.

Parents of young people in the Foundation and outside observers charge that members are poorly clothed and fed, ill-housed and overworked while Tony and Susan live in luxury off their labors. Susan Alamo's daughter, Mrs. Chris Mick, who says she is in hiding from her mother because she fears for her life, confirms the parents' accusations that the Alamos are exploiting the young people for their own profit. She testified at the 1974 California Senate Subcommittee Hearings into Religious Cults that "My mother makes a fortune at this organization. An absolute raving fortune."

Mrs. Kitchener likens the group's internal self-discipline system to Hitler's storm troopers. The Alma townspeople, who fear the Alamos, say the young people appear to be in a "trancelike state." One Alma man says, "They'll talk to you if you're in their place of business, but outside they won't even look at you. They pass each other on the street and don't even look at each other."

Parents complain that their children were forced into joining as well as staying in the group by threats of eternal damnation. Former member Bob Brownell testified at the 1974 California hearings. He said, "You were not allowed to leave. You were instilled from the moment you got there . . . that anyone who leaves is a backslider." They were taught, he says, that leaving the Foundation is the worst possible sin, "that your head will be severed from your shoulders." Some parents claim that their children are "brainwashed" into believing they had been hopeless drug addicts and are "force-fed" identical stories about being "rescued" from destitution by the Alamos.

Parents contend that their children are made to believe that their own families are in league with the devil and are forced to cut ties with them. Any contact between them is hostile. Ida Kitchener relates a conversation she had with her son after she convinced the Arkansas police to get him to telephone her. Bob was

> full of venom and rage. He had never spoken to me this way before. He became very abusive because he was certain that I was trying to hurt the Foundation, and nothing I said could abate his anger. When I told him that I only wanted to see him, he replied that if I came to Arkansas he would have me destroyed, and that I was never to write or speak to him again. After speaking to other parents, I am convinced that Bob was programmed to say these terrible things.

The Alamos claim Foundation members are well cared for and happy and for perhaps the first time in their lives productive and self-sufficient. They contend Mrs. Alamo's daughter is simply out to get revenge on her mother, that the media has given them bad publicity, and that all criticism of them is rooted in a widespread "Communist conspiracy."

A few Foundation members have been removed from the group by court-ordered conservatorships which grant parents temporary custody on the grounds that the young people are mentally incompetent. Conflicts between distraught parents and the Alamos came to a climax in the summer of 1977. On June 17, the parents of four Foundation members obtained an Arkansas court order giving them temporary thirty-day custody of their children through a conservatorship. The four children, Mark Cuneen, Joseph Orlando, Angelo Bennetti, and Arlene Gonzales, appeared at police headquarters to be turned over to the parents as directed by the court, but for unknown reasons were allowed to leave the police station. The parents, who had planned to have them deprogrammed at a nearby motel, went to see the children at the Alamo restaurant where they worked. They were thrown out of the restaurant, as were reporters; Mrs. Cuneen charges she was assaulted by six men who twisted her arm and threw her against a wall. The parents returned to their motel and were afraid to leave it because they were picketed by two dozen Foundation members and the Alamos. The four children filed a $2 million suit against their parents and the deprogrammer, alleging infringement of their civil rights. Because of lack of funds the group of parents has ceased all attempts to get their children out of the group.

Since the Alamo Foundation is a corporation involved in interstate commerce, the United States Department of Labor has filed suit against it, charging it with not paying its workers the minimum wage, not compensating them for overtime work, and not keeping certain required records.

The Divine Light Mission

In the spring of 1973, Rennie Davis, a New Leftist antiwar activist and member of the famous Chicago Seven, called a news conference to announce that "there is now a practical way to fulfill all the dreams of the movement of the early sixties and seventies. There's a practical method to end poverty, racism, sexism, imperialism." He had become, he explained, a follower of the revolutionary teachings of Guru Maharaj Ji, Spiritual Master of the Divine Light Mission. Said Davis, "I would cross the planet on my hands and knees to touch his toe."

The short, rotund, noncharismatic Indian guru, whose real name is Prem Pal Singh Rawat, seems an unlikely figure to inspire such passionate commitment. But when his father, the wealthy and high-born Shri Hans Ji, who had preached among India's poor since 1960, died, the eight-year-old boy was already widely known for his unusual spiritual qualities. His mother chose him over three older brothers to continue her husband's successful Divine Light Mission.

In 1971 an American businessman on a trip to India was impressed by the thirteen-year-old guru and persuaded him to come to the United States. With the help of financial backing from the businessman's friends in Boulder, Colorado, and the most up-to-date public relations techniques, Maharaj Ji caused a sensation.

He attracted many young members of the counter-culture. By 1973 there were forty to fifty thousand followers called "premies" (an Indian word meaning "lover of God") in the United States. About six hundred of them lived full-time in the Divine Light Mission communal ashrams ("shelters"), with three hundred in the Denver commune. The movement boasted 480 centers in thirty-eight countries around the world and had an estimated 6 million followers in India alone.

The Mission incorporated in Colorado as a tax-exempt church and grew into a multi-million-dollar a year business enterprise. According to Michael Bergman, the group's Executive Financial Director, between January and June, 1973, its business concerns grew 800 percent. They invested in real estate, operated printing businesses, a band, and restaurants. Income came also from large gifts, tithing of all members, and from the assets turned over by premies who lived in the ashrams. Maharaj Ji rode in a green Rolls-Royce, a Mercedes 600, a Lotus sportscar, and on several motorcycles. The group owned houses in London, New York, and Denver. In 1974 the Mission purchased the four-acre Anacapa View estate in Malibu, California, for Maharaj Ji and his new bride. The mansion on the ocean with swimming pool and tennis court cost half a million dollars.

Unmarried premies living in ashrams must be celibate. They cannot drink alcohol, use tobacco or drugs, eat meat, poultry or eggs, but are allowed coffee, tea, milk, and dairy products such as cheese. The followers take a vow of poverty during the elaborate initiation ceremony. They are encouraged to give all of their money and possessions to the Mission, to turn over nearly all of their subsequent income, and to work for the Mission without pay. Since most premies are transient they usually abandon school and career to work at any odd job they can find in the area. Even those premies who do not live in an ashram must maintain close ties with the Mission centers and go there frequently to discuss their beliefs.

Most followers send their children to regular public schools, but the Mission runs an accredited elementary school in Denver, the Unity School, which is based on Rudolph Steiner's progressive Waldorf method.

The Divine Light Mission's recruiting techniques are "soft-sell." They recruit members primarily through newspapers and yellow-pages advertising and by "personal witnessing" in which premies speak glowingly of their new-found peace and happiness since "receiving Knowledge" from Maharaj Ji or one of the Mahatmas or Prime Disciples designated by the guru to dispense "Knowledge."

This "receiving of Knowledge" is at the heart of the Divine Light Mission. It is a practical experience, not an abstract idea or theology. The Guru teaches that the mind or rational thought is the enemy of the experience because it stands in the way of attaining bliss. The "Knowledge" one receives from Maharaj Ji frees one from the "devil" mind. "Receiving Knowledge" can transform a skeptic who has become disillusioned with reason and with political ideologies; it can make him "see, hear, and taste the divine." Knowledge can change the world and bring it peace. Only Maharaj Ji has this Knowledge and possesses the key to help others get in touch with God, the source of all. Only the guru can make them realize that the entire universe is "one great field of energy."

"Knowledge" is given, and the candidate becomes a premie, in a secret initiation ceremony that lasts from five to fifteen hours. First the candidate fills out a "knowledge card," which includes a detailing of his financial assets. The Mahatma gives a lecture and all bow and prostrate themselves before the guru's photograph, after which the room is darkened and he demonstrates the Mission's four techniques. In the first, "Divine Light," the Mahatma presses on the candidate's eyeballs until pressure on the optic nerve causes him to see flashes of light. During the second, "Nectar," the person's head is tilted back and he curls the top of his tongue into the back of the throat until he tastes nasal drippings. In the third technique, "The Word," a secret mantra for meditation is given and a rhythmic breathing pattern established. In the fourth, "Divine Harmony," the candidate plugs his ears with his fingers until he hears a sort of buzzing sound. Mission members insist that a physical description of these techniques cannot convey the quality of the mystical experience.

Receiving Knowledge is only the first step for the new premie. They compare it to planting a seed that must be nurtured. The Knowledge experience must be followed up by sessions of "Satsang" ("company of truth") during which the leader and the premies talk extensively about Knowledge and commitment to Mission life. Premies must also meditate formally, seated, for at least two hours a day. Many meditate far more; some claim they meditate constantly while doing other things.

The wild growth of the Divine Light Mission peaked by the end of 1973. Mission officials blamed a bad press. Expectations for "Millennium '73," billed as the "most significant event in the history of humanity," were too high. Premies predicted the festival would bring one thousand years of peace and there were even rumors that a UFO would land in the Houston Astrodome's parking lot. The three-day festival was held in the Astrodome on November 9, 10, and 11, dates which coincided with meaningful astrological configurations. But the actual event was disappointing. Although they had expected 100,000 followers, only fifteen to twenty thousand attended; an earlier Billy Graham rally in the Astrodome had drawn 66,000. The Divine Light Mission was left with a huge debt. Further bad publicity ensued when Maharaj Ji married his secretary, former airline stewardess Marolyn Lois Johnson, in 1974. The guru's mother was so upset over the marriage and her son's opulent life-style that she disowned him and designated one of his older brothers to take over the Mission. Maharaj Ji fought his brother in courts in India and they finally agreed that he would retain control of the United States

Mission while his mother and brother headed the operation in India.

In order to reduce its debts the Mission closed down and consolidated its business enterprises. By 1976 all but five of the largest ashrams were closed down. Full-time members, by then only about three hundred in the United States, two hundred of them in Denver, scattered into communal apartments. With the reduction of the number of premies living in ashrams who donated their incomes to the Mission, there was a corresponding reduction in the movement's income. But observers estimate that the movement is still worth about $5 million.

With its "flower children" followers growing older, DLM spokesman Joe Anctil announced in August, 1976, that the Mission would change its image. Extravagant "trappings" such as the parade automobiles would be eliminated. The movement would be decentralized and run more democratically, with each Mission branch autonomous and the international headquarters merely a "coordinating and communications body." No longer would devotees kiss Maharaj Ji's feet at Mission Festivals or think of him as God incarnate, the Perfect Master; rather they would look upon him as simply a human being with important teachings. The number of Mahatmas empowered to give Knowledge was reduced from 2,000 to seven; three of the seven were now Americans, whereas previously all Mahatmas had been Indians. With a decline in the number of Mission businesses in which premies could work, full-time devotees were encouraged to take jobs in the outside world.

According to the Mission's own estimates there are presently about ten to fifteen thousand premies in the United States and 1.2 million throughout the world. In March, 1979, the Mission announced it was moving its national offices to Miami, Florida, and keeping only legal offices and a small staff in Denver.

Even though its wealth and membership is reduced, the Divine Light Mission's ideas and practices still hold great power over its premies, and critics contend that for those whose entire lives are tied up in the group the Mission presents all of the dangers of other cults. They charge that while the premies lead a life of renunciation and poverty, Maharaj Ji enjoys a life of pleasure and luxury. Said one man in Malibu: "I've seen people living out of dumpsters and shoplifting at local markets just so they can stay out here and be near him [Maharaj Ji]." Another Malibu resident told the *Los Angeles Times*: "I am irritated. I see him coming down the hill in his Mercedes while these kids live on next to nothing."

The premies must pledge their first allegiance to the Mission and obedience to Maharaj Ji. Declares one woman in the Malibu Mission: "This isn't my body. This isn't my flesh. If Maharaj Ji wants to take care of my body, that's fine. The most important thing is to obey the Perfect Master." Robert Mishler, the Mission's former president, reports that the guru often humiliates premies. "He would have followers strip in front of others." He says that Maharaj Ji once poured a can of oil over a premie who was servicing his car. Mishler and the Mission's former vice president, John Hand, Jr., accuse Maharaj Ji of sexual and physical assaults on his followers. Mishler says the guru frequently beat premies with his fist or a cane and that he (Mishler) was "kneed in the groin once for no reason at all."

Critics believe the basic idea of the movement—that rational thought prevents one from reaching God—can be dangerous. They say the Divine Light Mission meditation methods wear down the mind and can cause anxiety, release fears normally kept in check by reason, destroy faith in one's own judgment, and weaken will power and creativity. The Mission's meditation method of concentrating intensely on something (a mantra or a noise) can, they maintain, actually negate feelings and thought. Some critics contend that the meditation method is designed to do so: when anxiety and negative thoughts or feelings creep into the mind, meditation blocks the conflict. One former premie told Conway and Siegelman that this blockage of disturbing thoughts can become second-nature if one meditates enough. For him meditation became "a conditioned response." He kept doing it without trying even after he was deprogrammed, and he reports it took him months to rebuild his thinking capacity.

Barbara Fabe, who was deprogrammed from the Mission, believes she was brainwashed through constant repetition and bombardment of the group's doctrine. "You are doing something that rationally you know is nuts," she explains. "It's the suggestion . . . It is reinforced every time . . . They're salesmen, but more than salesmen, they're adept at mind control." She is convinced she would have done anything Guru Maharaj Ji told her to do. "I was programmed," she asserts. "I was not acting of my own free will . . . I believe I was under hypnosis."

The two former Divine Light Mission high officials, Mishler and Hand, fear there is a potential for violence in the group. They relate that after the Guyana tragedy Maharaj Ji showed behavior similar to that of the Reverend Jim Jones. They claim the guru had spoken frequently of building a city similar to Jonestown and in 1974 Mishler actually filed incorporation papers in Colorado for the formation of the City of Love and Light Unlimited, Inc. An attempt to build the community near San Antonio, Texas, failed in 1975.

Mishler reports also that after Maharaj Ji saw the movie, *The Godfather,* he became fascinated with the criminal underworld and set up a ten-member security unit called the "World Peace Corps." Armed with rifles and handguns, the security force lives at the Malibu estate and travels with the guru to protect him and, says Mishler, "to control members" who are overwhelmed by emotion during his personal appearances.

Church of Armageddon/Love Family

In January, 1972, two young men died after sniffing toluene, a solvent used industrially to break down rubber, with plastic bags over their heads in a Church of Armageddon "rite of breathing." According to witnesses, the group's leader, Love . Israel, sought no medical help for the victims but instead told members to keep praying and the bodies would rise again in three days. He assured his followers that the young men had been disobedient and their deaths were punishment for their sins.

Love Israel, who was Paul Erdman, a former real-estate agent with a record of drug-related arrests, founded the commune in 1969 in order, he claims, to fulfill the New Testament as it was revealed to him. His "Love Family" now has about two hundred fifty to three hundred members. Although centered in Seattle, Washington, it has branch colonies in Alaska and Hawaii. The group owns nine houses on Queen Ann Hill in Seattle, Washington, a 160-acre ranch in Washington, a $250,000 house in Hawaii, land in Alaska, a cargo ship, lumber mill, cannery, and an airplane.

Church of Armageddon members lead starkly regimented lives. They are not allowed to go anywhere alone, are isolated from clocks, radio, television, and newspapers, can have no sexual relationships or friendships with people outside the group, have their incoming and outgoing mail censored, and cannot carry money or drive automobiles. Renouncing the past, they are taught that the Love Family is now their real family, and are encouraged to cut off contact with their parents. If they do write to them, they address their parents by their first names rather than as "mother" or "father."

New members are baptized by total immersion which symbolizes the death of one's past self and past life. New members cast off their old names and adopt new "virtue names" such as Charity, Faith, and Courage, characteristics they must then try to emulate. Because they are one Family, all members take on the common surname "Israel." (The group also renames the days of the week, months, and years according to biblical patterns.) In addition, at the time of initiation the new member must sign a "Last Will and Testament" in which he declares himself "dead to the past." They give all worldly possessions to the group, grant power of attorney to Love Israel and agree that if they die their body cannot undergo an autopsy.

Love Israel often declares legal marriages of those wed before joining the group to be over and "bonds" together members according to his wishes or those of other men in the group. Women generally have little voice in the arranged liaisons. Professor Ronald Enroth states in his book, *Youth, Brainwashing, and the Extremist Cults,* that "theoretically" Love Israel has "sexual access to any woman in the group." Joyce and Robert Paris, whose son, Tom, spent five years in the Church of Armageddon, say the women obeyed Love Israel completely and worshiped him. The women are subservient to the men. There are reports of sexual abuse, and some women lose their sexuality altogether because of poor physical health.

Some who have observed the communes report that the members appear to be well cared for and happy. However, former members assert adherents are badly mistreated. Small children are isolated and locked in closets when they misbehave or appear to be unhappy or ungrateful. They are harshly disciplined by spankings with a stick on the orders of Love Israel, who believes giving love to children spoils them and that disciplining them gets Satan out of their bodies. A former Love Family member told a newspaper reporter that "one little boy was afraid and crying and a couple of adults stuffed dirty washcloths into his mouth until the corner of his mouth ripped and began bleeding."

Other witnesses testified in a 1974 federal trial in Seattle, Washington, in which deprogrammer Ted Patrick was acquitted of the charge of kidnaping Kathe Crampton from the group, that adults as well as children were mistreated. One member received forty blows with a two-foot long stick while the others watched because he had had sexual relations with a woman outside of the Family. Former members report that in one of the groups's religious ceremonies some of the Family sat in a circle holding hands, with one of them holding a piece of metal plugged into an electric outlet. The current was turned on and it ran through their bodies. According to these observers, tolerance to the electric current was a test of faith.

Former members testified in the Patrick trial that one cult

elder said, "it might one day become necessary to kill some-one for disciplinary reasons." Tom Paris believes members would do whatever Love Israel ordered, "up to and including suicide and murder." Another former adherent confirms she "heard people say they would kill for Love Israel. They have [Charles] Manson's view of life." Paris alleges the group has a small arsenal of guns and knives and that Family members march and are put through military drills.

Love Israel maintains the body doesn't really need food be-cause God will keep it alive, and so both adults and children in the group are undernourished and sometimes denied food. One former member reports that they sometimes ate popcorn for dinner and that she "looked like a skeleton right out of a concentration camp." If a small child moves toward food or acts hungry while being fed, Enroth writes, the food is taken away. A former member told him that one child was not fed for three days. Members are often inadequately clothed. Ill-ness is seen as a sign of lack of faith and hence the members receive poor medical treatment, if any.

Tom Paris maintains that the group uses "all kinds of drugs, whatever comes along" as rewards and in religious cere-monies. The toluene sniffing ritual was discontinued after two followers died, but former members report hashish is used in a religious ritual during which adherents hyperventilate. Mem-bers smoke marijuana, bake marijuana cookies, and manufac-ture hallucinogenic substances from flowers in their garden. Love Israel has acknowledged that he believes drugs are sacramental, that they break down barriers between people, and help to bring his followers closer together.

Critics charge that the Church of Armageddon uses danger-ous indoctrination techniques such as awakening members twice every night, which interrupts their sleep patterns. Ar-mageddon leaders call this practice "nightwatch" and claim they do it in order to assure their members of their love and concern for them and to see if they are having any visions or bad dreams. In an account of his family's attempts to get his brother, Douglas, out of the group, Philip Fraiman relates that he believes Douglas and the other Love Family members are "brainwashed":

> . . . our brother had already changed radically. His eyes were glassy and his conversation was without emotion or spontaneity. With a quizzical smile fixed on his face, he repeatedly attributed his newly-found enlightenment to Jesus Christ as represented by someone called "Love Israel" . . . Doug was not unusual. All the people there appeared to have the same mannerisms, dress, speech, and answers. It was as though every one of these souls had been refabricated into a facsimile of the charismatic cult leader.

(A court order removed Douglas Fraiman from the group in May, 1976. But after being pressured by church members to come back he returned and is still in the group.) The Paris's, of Xenia, Ohio, confirm that their son, Tom, and other church members spoke in a monotone. They are convinced that there is a "high degree of mind control" in the group.

Very few leave the communes and those who do leave have great difficulty readjusting to the outside world. Yale psychiatrist Robert Jay Lifton believes the Love Family "is one of the most extreme of the religious cults," and that the effects of its harmful indoctrination methods "could become irreversible."

Body of Christ

On April 26, 1979, a small private airplane carrying Sam Fife and three of his Body of Christ followers crashed in Guatemala. All on board were killed. Fifty-four-year-old Fife was enroute to visit the group's Quiche Theological Institute and one of its settlements in Guatemala.

Fife, a Southern Baptist minister, was teaching Bible studies in North Canton, Ohio, when he, C.E. ("Buddy") Cobb, and Dr. James Meffen founded the group in 1962. It is also known as "The End Time Ministry," "The Movement," and "The Body." Today there are seven to ten thousand members in two dozen communes they call "wilderness farms" located in Ohio, Texas, Georgia, Florida, Mississippi, Alaska, British Columbia in Canada, Guatemala, and Peru. According to a *New York Times* report, the group owns "a fleet of planes" so the outposts can be reached.

Leaders insist there is no single organization called "The Body of Christ." They say the groups are really autonomous, separate entities with no official connection. Settlements and branches have various names. The Dallas group is known as "The Dallas Northtown Church," a major settlement near Eupora, Mississippi, is known as "The Church of Sapa," and many are called simply "Christian Ministries." However, two critics of the group, Dr. Meffen, who broke with his co-founders in the 1970s and left the organization, and former member Charlene Hill, disagree. Meffen and Hill say the members think of themselves as one group in fellowship and speak of themselves as "The Body of Christ" when they are together.

Adherents study and follow the teachings of Sam Fife and Donald Barnhouse, the Body of Christ's other major theologian before his death. They believe the Bible should guide their lives. They forecast an impending period of "Great Tribulation" and believe it is their task to prepare to be the new leaders in this "end of time" and to ready places where people can fend for themselves after the great disaster has cut off electricity, food supplies, and other necessities. They raise animals and grow their own food on wilderness farms in an attempt to become self-sufficient. According to Dr. Meffen the members speak of themselves as "manifested sons of God" and believe that once they have perfected themselves "Christ will be manifested through them." They speak in tongues, practice faith healing, and believe in demon possession.

Recruitment is subtle; critics Meffen and Hill say they find people who are unhappy and channel them into the Body of Christ and also "infiltrate existing churches and Bible study groups." Members live austerely, with poor clothing and no radio or television. They must turn over their property to the group and many older followers even sign over their pensions.

Critics charge that families are broken up if one spouse joins a communal settlement without the other. The Body of Christ has been named in child-abuse and child-desertion cases. Charlene Hill, who with her husband and three children spent eight years in the group, reports that the children are disciplined severely. She has in her possession a tape recording of her daughter relating that she was spanked "hard" if she didn't answer questions correctly in school.

Mrs. Hill asserts the group teaches that it is not wrong to "distort the truth when talking to reporters." Former members believe they were brainwashed. Hill reports that members must constantly listen on headsets to tapes and read speeches by Fife and Barnhouse. Shortly before Mrs. Hill left, the group told her she was possessed by demons and tried to beat them out of her. They tied her to a bed, whipped her with a belt and submerged her in a tub of cold water. Another former member, Shari Smith, relates that she was beaten with a wooden paddle and that rebellious members were tied to beds, chairs, or the floor and thrown into cold showers with their clothes on until they repented. She was once kept in a cold shower for four and a half hours.

The Body of Christ came under public scrutiny when the Reverend John Hinson, one of its leaders, was convicted in 1977 on charges of kidnaping in Mississippi. Hinson was sentenced to ten years in prison, but he appealed and the conviction was overturned.

The Children of God

The Children of God call themselves also "Family of Love." They preach that God is love, he loves you, and you can be saved if you love. But, according to its critics, the group also teaches hatred.

Former Children of God members report that the "Children" are taught that their parents are the enemy and embody Satan's evil. They hate the United States ("America the Whore"), its economy, and its entire establishment "system," which they believe is doomed. One of the primary objects of hatred is Israel and the Jews. Children of God literature is replete with old anti-Semitic charges that the Jews, spurned by God because they have refused to accept Jesus, control banks and the media and are Christ killers. In graphic cartoon literature they accuse the Israelis of wanting to exterminate all Palestinians and to start another war in the Middle East. According to a March, 1979, B'nai Brith Anti-Defamation League study, David Berg, the Jewish-born founder and leader of the group, has also made anti-Catholic statements. In a letter entitled "Arrivederci Roma" Berg writes:

> We are now beginning to invade the Catholic countries of the world and we are going to have to be pro-Catholic . . . Go partake of their little Eucharist, go kneel with them in their chapels . . . They don't know anything else . . . Play along with them if that pleases them . . . what is it if you can act like a clown? In other words, join a circus!

The group's anti-Semitism and Third World ties are cemented by its close relationship with Libya's Colonel Moammar Kaddafi, which goes back to 1973. They consider Kaddafi to be "one of God's chosen ones" as a world leader, and he responds that the Children of God are "the new prophets." They look upon Kaddafi as a Christ- or Mohammed-like Messiah figure, even calling him "Godhafi." The group receives extensive moral support and financial help from Libya, and a large new Children of God spiritual center is being built in Tripoli, Libya.

The Children of God predict that the world will end in 1993. Signaled by a final Middle Eastern Armaggedon, America will fall first to Communism, then the rest of the world will be destroyed. But the "Children" will be the remnant, the new nation that will rule the world until Jesus' final return.

In the mid-1960s David Brandt Berg left his job as minister of a small, Baptist church in Arizona. He moved his family to southern California and went to work for television evangelist Fred Jordan. In the fall of 1968 Berg started working with "hippies," mostly drug addicts, and founded "Teens for Christ" in Huntington Beach, Los Angeles. The group soon became known as "Revolutionaries for Christ." A journalist dubbed them "Children of God," and they adopted that name. The small group grew rapidly, and, aided by extensive media coverage, was in the forefront of the 1960s Jesus-People movements.

Fred Jordan let them live on his ranches near Mingus, Texas, and in Coachilla, California. But in October, 1971, Jordan and Berg had a falling out, apparently over administrative and financial matters, and Jordan evicted them. (Jordan later claimed he gave the group $98,000 in cash and spent half a million dollars promoting it.) The Children of God began to wander around the country in small groups, setting up temporary communes.

In 1972 Berg closed many of his communes in the United States because, he says, he believed America was doomed. In order to spread the gospel he moved most of the Children to Europe, particularly to England and Holland. However, critics maintain Berg fled the United States to escape from growing criticism. In 1974, New York Attorney General Louis Lefkowitz issued a scathing report on the Children of God; most of Berg's followers left the United States just prior to its publication.

The group now claims to have eight thousand full-time disciples who have, according to Berg, made over 2 million converts to Christ. There are over eight hundred Children of God communes throughout the world. A 1978 issue of its publication *New Nation News* proclaims their communes are "in seventy-four countries on every continent." The group is apparently growing rapidly. They are particularly strong in South America, Europe—England, Italy, and Holland—and Australia. Many of the members in these colonies are young

Americans, and the Lefkowitz Report indicates there may still be some Children-of-God groups left in the United States, operating under aliases such as "Contact Jesus," "The Christian Faith Association," and "The Toronto Christian Truth Ministry."

The communes, called "colonies," consist of six to twelve members who are led by a "shepherd" or married "shepherd couple." When the group grows larger than twelve it divides and forms a new one which is then directed by this "mother colony" until it becomes strong enough to support itself and develop its own leadership. Some colonies travel constantly, others remain in one place. Each colony has a specific function. Some write and publish Children of God material, others translate it, and some are school or administrative colonies. In order to mute parental criticism, they will not accept anyone under eighteen years of age, so minors live in "catacombs" colonies. Children of God disciples in prisons and on United States military bases abroad are also in "catacombs" colonies, as they cannot live as full-fledged communal members.

There are eight levels of colonies. At each ascending level there is a council that presides over the level below it. Two or three colonies form a district, headed by a district shepherd or shepherd couple. A former Children of God leader describes the complex organization:

> Three districts form a region, headed by a regional shepherd. Three regions constitute a bishopric, presided over by a bishop, and three bishoprics constitute an archbishopric, headed by an archbishop. Three archbishoprics constitute a prime ministry, ruled over by a prime minister. At the time I left there were four prime ministers in the COG. They are members of the board of directors called "The King's Counselors." It's a pyramid type of government, ruled from the top down.

Berg claims that through his pyramid organization he has dispersed administrative authority, but critics maintain he still rules with an iron hand.

All Children except those in the catacombs colonies must live in the communes and fully devote their lives to the group. They take on biblical names and give up all secular work so they can be "100 percent for God." No liquor or drugs are allowed.

The leaders must approve marriages and often arrange them, sometimes without the bride and groom knowing ahead of time that they are to be married or who the partner will be. They encourage the couple to have children so that the group can propagate quickly, and the birth rate is high. Formerly, women did not go to hospitals to bear children, but now more are being born in hospitals and medical care in general for the Children has improved. Although younger children can stay with their parents at night, they do not usually live with them and may even be sent to another colony if their parents' commune doesn't have an adequate school. They teach them according to the Montessori method, but educate them only for the purpose of reading and studying the Bible, as Berg expresses contempt for education in his written teachings.

Women may have some positions of leadership as one half of a shepherd couple, but observers maintain that women are generally subservient to the men and are often sexually abused because of the unorthodox sexual mores of the group. One fourteen-year-old girl reports that she was raped after refusing to cooperate with the elders. Former members report extensive partner swapping among high-echelon disciples. Leaders order and orchestrate sexual orgies for all the Children. They order and, some observers maintain, carefully train women disciples to use their sexuality to recruit new members and solicit large donations. The Lefkowitz Report charges that Berg condones polygamy, incest, and sexual activity of minors. Witnesses of the New York State Frauds Bureau investigation which was the basis for the Lefkowitz Report testified that many minors in Children of God communes were pregnant. Other critics charge that Berg condones lesbianism

The Children eat adequately except in the poorer areas of

the world, but the average disciple lives in poverty while the leaders live in comfort and, some observers contend, in luxury. Berg, who is about sixty years old, reportedly lives in isolation on a large estate near Florence, Italy, donated by an Italian nobleman.

They get donations of money from merchants and other outsiders, even from parents who approve of them. They are taught to exploit the evil "system" fully and to extract as much as possible from it, such as free haircuts, eyeglasses, housing, food, and clothing. The Children have ties to a French singing group, "Les Enfants de Dieu," and own discotheques called "Poor Boy Clubs" in major cities throughout the world. They market posters, tapes, record albums, coffee cups, and tee-shirts bearing Children of God slogans. They make and sell "yokes," emblems that hang around the neck. The Lefkowitz Report concludes that "monies are directed to the key leaders for their personal use and enjoyment."

The members must turn over all their funds and possessions. The belongings are either sold or used by the commune. Some have donated extensive property, such as the large farm and wine-producing estate, Poggiosecco, in the Florentine hills. It was given to the group by a wealthy Italian, Emanuele Canevaro, now a disciple married to a prominent Children of God leader who calls herself Queen Rachel.

Most income comes from sales of massive amounts of Children of God literature. Every member must "witness"— peddle literature on the streets—six to ten hours a day. In 1975 these sales grossed over $5 million. The group claims the literature is not profitable, but a former leader says that the income from "witnessing" is nearly all pure profit, and most of it goes to Berg and other top leaders. The Children of God also sell brochures, books, and their *New Nation News* magazine. But the most profitable item is "Mo Letters," communications from David Berg who is also known as "Uncle David," "Uncle Mo," or "Mo." Many millions of copies of the more than five hundred "Mo Letters" in existence have been sold. These "Mo Letters' are the only contact lower-echelon Children have with the reclusive Berg, and they look forward to his communications with great excitement and joy. These letters have gradually become more important to the group than the Bible; Berg has declared that their authority surpasses that of the Scriptures. Not all are intended for public consumption or for the average disciple, but some of the private letters have fallen into critics' hands.

Berg writes on a variety of subjects such as "America the Whore" and "The Green Pig" (the American dollar), but primarily he writes about sex. He counsels female followers to be "Happy Hookers for Jesus," admonishing them to use seductive charm to get more members. In a "Mo Letter" entitled "God's Love Slave" he recounts how he gave his wife to many men and then relished in a detailed description of the activities. A 1978 "Mo Letter" entitled "Come on, Ma, Burn Your Bra!"—a comic book with near-pornographic illustrations—equates spiritual salvation and God's love to sexual experience and assures readers that sexual expression is a form of God's love—

> So, if you think there's something wrong with sex and you should be ashamed of your body, then there's something wrong with GOD and you should be ashamed of HIM and US as well! We have a SEXY GOD and a SEXY RELIGION with a very SEXY LEADER and an extremely SEXY YOUNG FOLLOW-ING! So if you don't like SEX, you'd better get out while you can still save your BRA! SALVATION sets us FREE from the curse of clothing and the shame of NAKEDNESS. We're as free as ADAM and EVE in the GARDEN before they ever sinned! If you're NOT, you're not fully SAVED . . . COME ON, MA! BURN YOUR BRA! BE LIBERATED TONIGHT!*

Are Children of God recruits "brainwashed" into joining and staying with the group? A former prominent leader, Jack Wasson, says "no" but some former disciples report they were never left alone, were closely guarded, forced to read

*"Come on Ma, Burn your Bra!" A brochure by Moses David, February 1978; published by The Family of Love, CP 748, 00100, Rome, Italy, p.6.

and memorize Bible passages for at least twelve hours a day and to attend long and exhausting Bible-study sessions. Loud-speakers constantly blared biblical quotations even when they tried to sleep. In *All Gods Children* Parke and Stoner relate that former disciples report that they had to earn food and rest by memorizing Bible quotations. One retarded boy who was unable to memorize was "simply not fed for days. His parents finally found him in a dehydrated, debilitated condition. He had lost more than twenty pounds in a few days."

Ex-members report that the Children of God has guards who are sometimes armed and that the leaders made them afraid to leave the group. They were told that God would "strike them dead," that he would punish them for going back into the evil world. A leader told one former member that there were "kids who went insane or dropped dead or were in car accidents after they left the Children of God." Former members report that they were allowed no privacy, and that, if they were per-mitted to make telephone calls, the phones were often tapped or taped, outgoing and incoming mail was intercepted, and they were physically as well as mentally coerced. Sarah Berg, David Berg's former daughter-in-law, was beaten with "a two-by-four" by her husband only two weeks before her baby was born because of disobeying orders.

Some parents who have deprogrammed their children from the group maintain their appearance had been transformed, especially their eyes which had a glassy, dazed look. One mother contends that even after her child left the group a post-hypnotic effect could be triggered simply by reading the Bible.

Parents assert that the group prevents them from finding their children. They believe the Children take on biblical names to make it more difficult for the parents to trace them. Some whose children are in colonies overseas have not heard from them for years and do not even know if their children are still alive.

Critics contend that the Children of God have replaced wor-ship of God with worship of David Brandt Berg and that what began as a fundamentalist Christian sect has been transformed into a heretical, anti-Christian cult. Berg has buried the Christian doctrine of love under an avalanche of hatred, rebellion, and bitterness. His doctrine of "salvation by sex" has led to promiscuous sexual activity. Jack Wasson says that Berg claims to receive revelations from dozens of occult sources which he calls "spiritual counselors," including the spirits of Joan of Arc, Merlin the Magician, Martin Luther, and William Jennings Bryan and that Berg also claims to have sexual relations with spirits.

In February, 1972, some parents in San Diego formed FREECOG (Free Our Children from the Children of God), which coordinates their battles against the group. Other parents who believe their children have found purpose and happiness started THANKCOG (Thankful Parents and Friends of the Children of God) in Dallas, Texas, in 1972.

Police raided the Poggiosecco estate in Italy in 1975 but found no evidence of law breaking. Berg and other leaders have been in no serious legal trouble. After the Children moved to England in 1972 Conservative Parliament-member John Hunt called for a governmental inquiry into the group. However, there were no arrests since the government could find no evidence that the Children were engaged in criminal activities.

The Church of Scientology

In August, 1979, an Oregon jury unanimously awarded a twenty-two-year-old former Scientologist from Montana $2,067,000 in damages from the Church of Scientology after a twenty-one day trial. Julie Christofferson Titchbourne recovered the damages on the charges of "outrageous conduct" and "common law fraud" (intentionally misrepresenting itself and not carrying out its promises that it would help her). The case was very unusual not only because of the size of the settlement but because it was one of the first major civil cases brought against the Scientologists. Some religious leaders were disturbed by the verdict, fearing that the decision imperils First Amendment guarantees of freedom of religion, but cult critics hail it as a major legal setback for all of the cults. Ron Wade, one of the attorneys who represented Mrs. Titchbourne, hailed her victory as a "real indictment of Scientology" and a breakthrough in the battle against the religious cults in the legal arena.

The attention given to this case symbolizes the intense controversy that has surrounded Scientology since it began in 1950 when former science-fiction and adventure-story writer Lafayette Ronald Hubbard published a book entitled *Dianetics: The Modern Science of Mental Health.* Hubbard's science of "Dianetics" spread quickly in the early 1950s from his Phoenix, Arizona, base. In 1954 Hubbard opened the Founding Church of Scientology in Washington, D.C. and in 1955 incorporated his ideas as a religion. Today church officials boast 4 to 5 million members, with twenty-two churches and one hundred missions in thirty-three countries. They claim there are 3 million Scientologists in the United States and 236,000 in England.

In 1959 Hubbard moved the church's headquarters to a 57-acre estate in England called Saint Hill Manor in East Grinstead, Sussex, an estate formerly owned by the Maharajah of Jaipur. Scientology owns six buildings in Hollywood, California, including the former Cedars of Lebanon Hospital complex purchased as seminary headquarters in February, 1977, for $5.5 million in cash. In 1976 the Scientologists paid several million dollars for the elegant old Fort Harrison Hotel in Clearwater, Florida, and converted it into a training center for high-level Scientologists called Flag Headquarters and since then have purchased six other buildings in downtown Clearwater. Ten percent of income from all Scientology churches and missions goes to the Mother Church in England.

Critics claim Scientology is not a religion. Scientologists insist their practical, self-help method is an authentic religion. Its ministers deliver sermons and perform weddings, christenings and funerals. They liken their concept of *Thetan,* a spirit that lives on after death in another body, to the religious notion of soul. Their idea of *Theta,* which is "the prime mover unmoved" could, they say, be thought of as God. In the March, 1979, issue of the Scientology newspaper, *Freedom,* Hubbard explains that "Scientology is a religious philosophy in its highest meaning, as it brings man to real knowingness of himself and truth." He claims Scientology is an extension of Buddhism and is a scientific technology that can "attain the goals set for man by Christ, which are wisdom, good health, and immortality." Hubbard promises that Scientology can sharpen mental awareness and ability to communicate with others, improve physical health, and heighten spiritual development.

These benefits occur through "processing" or "auditing" in a private session between a "pre-clear"—a person who has not yet attained "clear," which is the goal of auditing—and the Scientology auditor or processor. To work towards "clear" they use an E-Meter, which is a box with a dial connected to two cans. The E-Meter is a modified Wheatstone bridge, a device that measures electrical resistance. The "pre-clear" grasps the cans in his hands and the instrument electrically measures his response to a series of questions the auditor asks about his life. An overemotional reaction to a question indicates the "pre-clear" is disturbed. The goal of auditing is to bring answers to all questions within the range of "normal," which Scientology defines as the point where no strong emotional reaction is registered. The auditor asks the same questions over and over according to a prescribed pattern until the E-Meter registers the desired (normal) responses.

Scientologists believe that by bringing to the mind's surface and confronting emotionally charged experiences from the past, "engrams," the physical pain and emotional trauma associated with these experiences will disappear. These painful engrams, which are mental images created by the Thetan implanted on cell protoplasm, stem not only from childhood experiences but also from incidents that occurred while the person was in the womb. In order to become "clear" one must also remember "overts," which are mistakes made in the past. Recalling "overts" is similar to an act of confession. Engrams and overts are also carried over from past lives by the Thetan. Scientologists believe we have had many past lives going back perhaps trillions of years to other planets. We may not remember these past existences because the pain of the engrams has made us forget them. Auditing can allow us to remember the past lives and so can rid us of the pain of the engrams. When all engrams are eliminated the person becomes "clear." He can then move through higher stages of spiritual development, "Thetans," which range from "Operating Thetan One" to the highest, "Operating Thetan Six."

Pre-clears must also take "communications" courses, which consist of staring at others for perhaps several hours, and other special courses and lectures. They are required to buy many of Hubbard's books and other Scientology materials. They may purchase their own auditing equipment which, according to one Scientologist, costs about $400.

One need not abandon one's previous religion to become a Scientologist. The mission in Los Angeles is appealing to Israeli immigrants in that area by assuring them that they do not have to desert their Judaism in order to join the group called "The American Jewish Scientology Committee." By June, 1979, over two hundred Israelis had joined. The movement is growing in Israel where in 1977 about fourteen hundred elementary school children in Beersheba were given Scientology communications courses.

Children are audited according to special procedures if, according to one Scientologist, "they seem, for example, to be unhappy about something that happened in school that day." At least one educational organization, Applied Scholastics, located in Boston and California, has used Hubbard's methods in its program for tutoring high-school students, and claims it has coached Black Muslims and Methodist and Catholic churches in auditing.

L. Ron Hubbard is the church's only Prophet. There are many levels of ministers, including some auditors. A hierarchy of officials runs its branches and missions called "Orgs." Hubbard's wife, Mary Sue, is "Worldwide Guardian" of the church. Now in his late sixties, Hubbard lives in isolation reportedly either on a large ship called The Sea Org off the coast of Clearwater, Florida, or in an elegant penthouse at the top of the Clearwater headquarters. Occasionally rumors circulate that Hubbard is dead since he has not been seen in public for many years. One former Scientologist says Hubbard is very ill. A 1976 *Time Magazine* article said that during a lecture in Newark, New Jersey, in 1949, Hubbard counseled his audience saying that "Writing for a penny a word is ridiculous. If a man really wanted to make a million dollars, the best way would be to start his own religion."

Scientologists object to their movement's classification as a religious cult, but critics believe it is and they point first of all to the extremely high cost of attaining "clear." Fees for auditing and other Scientology courses, always called "donations," vary. In some places they range from fifty to seventy-five dollars for auditing sessions and classes, but Mrs. Mary Weeks, a Scientology critic in Portland, Oregon, reports that auditing in Portland costs $150 an hour. Some claim the average amount of money spent to try to become "clear" is $2,500; Mrs. Weeks says the average Scientologist in Portland spends $5,000. What may begin as a small financial outlay can grow into a massive financial investment involving life savings, trust funds, and commitment of future earnings. Several Scientologists report spending $10,000 to $15,000. One young man who recently left Scientology spent $23,000 in nine months and he had not even completed the second course. A few people have spent over $100,000 on Scientology.

Former Scientologists contend that when they attempted to stop their auditing they were very strongly discouraged. They were told that if they were unhappy with the results it was because they hadn't yet taken enough sessions, and they were pressured into signing up for still more. They were made to feel that if the auditing wasn't working it was their own fault— they hadn't been trying hard enough—and not that of Scientology.

Ex-members complain it is extremely difficult to get fees refunded if one is not satisfied with the auditing results. It is necessary to go through eleven or twelve church officials to get the money back. Mrs. Weeks reports it is easier now to get money back in Portland since Julie Titchbourne's courtroom victory. Scientology consumers are made to believe they have no legal recourse if they are dissatisfied, as they must sign a release form absolving Scientology of all legal liability when they begin auditing, when they leave the group, or when getting a refund. Although this document has no legal standing and will not hold up in a court, this procedure inhibits dissatisfied Scientologists from complaining.

Many Scientologists work very long hours for the group for little or no payment. Mrs. Weeks' son, Lynn, worked for the church seventeen hours a day on weekdays and Saturdays and twelve hours on Sundays. For this seven-day work week he was paid anywhere from nothing to forty dollars per week. Another former Scientologist says he worked an average of one hundred hours a week for an average of ten dollars in wages. Julie Titchbourne worked sixteen hours a day for four dollars per week.

One former Scientologist who calls herself "Sue Ann" reports she was under constant pressure to get new members and to encourage them to spend money on auditing and other courses. She maintains she was carefully drilled in how to recruit and control the new members. The Scientologists follow a four-step recruitment strategy. The first step is "contact," the initial friendly approach to the potential member. The second step is to "handle" the recruit, i.e., to overcome his reservations about Scientology. The third is to find the "ruin," or vulnerable area, of the potential member's life such as drugs, sex, a past crime, or incest. In the fourth step, "salvage," the recruiter assures the potential member that he knows other people who have overcome similar problems through Scientology.

Critics claim Scientology can gradually take over the lives of its followers. Most who are heavily involved in the movement live in Scientology centers or in houses or apartments with other Scientologists. Julie Titchbourne charged in her law suit that the church "alienated" her from her family. When her mother tried to get her out of the group, Scientologists ordered Julie to "disconnect" from her mother. Other former Scientologists relate they, too, were ordered to "disconnect" from their families and friends.

Ex-members maintain one cannot question church teachings and that the authoritarian Scientology leaders keep tight discipline by paramilitary methods. They explain that if one expresses personal doubt or questions church doctrine he can be censured by an "Ethics Officer" who lowers the wavering Scientologist's "ethics condition." (There are eleven "ethics conditions" called, in order from lowest to highest, Confusion, Treason, Enemy, Doubt, Liability, Nonexistence, Danger, Emergency, Normal, Affluence, and Power.) The errant Scientologist with a lowered "ethics condition" can raise himself to a higher level by performing humiliating "amends projects" such as writing out one hundred times that he was wrong, scrubbing floors, composing papers about his shortcomings, and gathering signatures on a petition from fellow members in order to be restored to the group's good graces. Dissenters are also threatened with being labeled a "suppressive person" or "enemy" with whom other Scientologists cannot speak or associate and who are subject to other punishments.

Mary Weeks charges people are kept in the group by guilt and fear. The Scientologist is vulnerable because the church discredits all other forms of psychotheraphy. "They tell you that you'll go insane if you leave," Mrs. Weeks explains. "They say you were insane before you came into it, you were sane while you were in it, and you'll be insane again if you leave." She believes that members fear that they will be blackmailed if they leave the group because of the personal secrets they have revealed in the auditing sessions. The auditors write down the secrets and keep them in files that are accessible to many Scientology officials. One former member agrees that members fear blackmail because

> you are coerced into divulging every secret you can possibly come up with . . . I had hundreds of hours of their "counseling" . . . a large portion of that was devoted to thinking up everything that not only I've done wrong, but anything that I could *imagine* that I've done wrong because they go into past lives . . . there's this extreme guilt.

Oregon attorney Ron Wade confirms that, during the Titchbourne trial, the Scientologists did indeed read aloud from private files of former Scientologists in an attempt to discredit them when they testified against the group.

Many former Scientologists believe they were hypnotized and their thoughts controlled during auditing. Julie Titchbourne, who joined the group when she was only seventeen years old, testified that she was brainwashed, that she became a "robot—despising my parents so much I thought about killing them." Garry McMurry, the lead attorney in her litigation against the church, describes Julie's experience with Scientology as "an Orwellian horror story" and says she was "programmed to be submissive, absolutely loyal and an absolutely mindless person."

Snapping authors Flo Conway and Jim Siegelman contend the auditing process can result in a mental condition similar to the "reduced awareness" found in other cults. Characteristics include a state of "narrowed or reduced cognition," blunted emotions, and even changes in physical appearance and posture. Their source, whom they call Howard Davenport—a false name—reports that the church tries to hide these physical changes by constant drilling to make the eyes look normal and the person appear natural and relaxed. These drills consist of set patterns of repeated orders given by the instructor and are designed to elicit the responses he desires. Howard explains:

One person acts as a coach and the other as the student, and he'll say, "Start!" and if you blink your eyes in an unnatural way, he'll say "Flunk! You blinked in an unnatural way. Start!" He coaches you for hours like that.

Conway and Siegelman believe prolonged auditing can cause people to experience "increasingly realistic hallucinations" so that eventually the individual can no longer "distinguish between what he is experiencing and what he is only imagining." Howard Davenport claims that the Scientologists can skillfully "transform awareness" and "create images of things in your mind that do not exist."

Critics charge that some former Scientologists have gone insane as a result of auditing and some have committed suicide because of it. Dr. Margaret Singer testified at the Titchbourne trial that Julie was suffering "from a stress response syndrome that has impared her recall, use of language, and concentration", and she still suffers from periods of dissociation and hallucinations. Dr. John G. Clark Jr. testified at the Oregon trial that Scientology is a dangerous and destructive cult that is "designed to tear apart the fabric of the mind." Its exercises are "utterly mutilating to a person's mind. Taken to its extreme, you can teach someone to kill."

The Church of Scientology is accused of harassing its critics in the courts. Since 1970 it has filed fifty-nine lawsuits in seven states against United States Government agencies including a $750 million lawsuit against the FBI. During the past ten years the Church of Scientology has filed more than one hundred lawsuits against publishers, authors, and others who have criticized it publicly. Assistant United States Attorney Raymond Banoun who prosecuted the government's case against the church declared in a July, 1979, article in *The National Law Journal* that he had "never run into such litigiousness before."

Paulette Cooper is one author who claims she was harassed by the church after Tower Publications, Inc. published her book, *The Scandal of Scientology,* in 1971. The church filed eighteen libel suits against her, each from different Scientology branches. The church maintains it had to file many separate suits because it is not centralized, but Herbert Rosedale, Tower's lawyer, contends Scientology is indeed centralized and that it filed multiple suits in order to harass Cooper (a separate lawyer would have to be retained for each suit because they were filed in different states, forcing her to pay eighteen lawyers' fees instead of one). In order to get a settlement, Miss Cooper promised she would not republish the book and signed a statement saying fifty-two passages in it were "misleading."

Critics say Scientologists harass them outside the courtroom also. One of the witnesses in the Titchbourne trial charges his life was threatened when he left the group and another claimed she was beaten after she stopped auditing. One of the alternate jurors in the Titchbourne proceedings, Marie Killman, reported to the judge during the trial that a man telephoned her and said, "If your findings are against the Scientology Church you will be killed." In a later telephone call the man threatened and said, "I will get you, I will get you." (Mrs. Killman was removed from the trial.) Paulette Cooper maintains she received anonymous death threats, her telephone was tapped during her legal battle with the church, and the Scientologists tried to frame her on charges of sending a bomb-threat letter to the church on her personal stationery containing her fingerprints which had been stolen from her apartment. She was indicted in May, 1973, on these charges; they were finally dropped when a lie detector test cleared her. Ron Wade asserts that the Scientologists tried to set up Julie Titchbourne on charges of kidnaping another Scientologist. Miss Cooper says the church sent letters to her neighbors telling them she had venereal disease and threatening her friends with legal actions. When FBI agents raided the church's headquarters in Washington, D.C. and Los Angeles in July, 1977, they seized personal files of Scientology critics kept by the church. One of these files was devoted to Paulette Cooper.

Entitled "P. C. Freakout," the file outlined plans for getting her declared mentally incompetent and put into either a mental institution or jail.

Documents seized in the 1977 raids on Scientology headquarters by FBI agents and released to the public in the fall of 1979 implicate the church, United States Government prosecutors allege, in other plots against its critics. These include the setting up in 1975 of a fake hit-and-run automobile accident involving the mayor, Gabriel Cezares, of Clearwater, Florida, after he had objected to the group's extensive purchases in that city, the infiltration by a Scientologist of the *Clearwater Sun* office to report on that newspaper's daily activities, the establishment of plans to discredit the editor and president of *St. Petersburg Times* and one of its reporters, the burglary of a law firm representing *St. Petersburg Times,* and the infiltration of *The Washington Post* newspaper office.

The church denies it harasses its critics, but the *New York Times* alleged in a January, 1979, series of articles on the cults that the group practices "black public relations" against its opponents. The newspaper obtained a May 30, 1974, confidential Scientology Board policy letter which outlined techniques for the "handling" of "hostile contacts." The letter instructed members to attack always, never to defend or deny charges in press releases, to investigate critics for "felonies or worse," "start feeding lurid, blood sex crime actual evidence . . . to the press," to "whisper a bad story, get a lawyer, threaten suit, totally discredit."

The Church of Scientology has many crusades. It claims to run a program called Narcanon for fighting drug abuse, and its "Committee to Reinvolve Ex-Offenders" rehabilitates former criminals and addicts. Scientologists have always been opposed to the medical profession, particularly to psychiatrists and the mental-health establishment. They believe psychiatrists torture patients and destroy their brains with electric shock treatments. In June, 1979, the group accused two psychiatrists in St. Paul, Minnesota, Dr. Francis Tyce and Dr. Malka Goodman, of unethical practices because of their participation in deprogrammings. Since 1969 the church's "Citizens Commission on Human Rights" has been probing abuses in mental hospitals in several states, including sixty cases of alleged abuses at the Creedmore Psychiatric Hospital in New York City.

The church's "National Commission on Law Enforcement and Social Justice" attacks Interpol, a French-based private police organization it contends has access to files of private citizens in every country, including many Scientologists. They accuse Interpol of anti-Semitism, of having ties to Hitler's Third Reich, and of providing an underground escape network for Nazis after World War II.

Scientologists have been battling the Federal Drug Administration since January, 1963, when FDA officials raided their headquarters, confiscated three tons of literature and E-Meters, and tried to declare the E-Meter ineffective. Scientologists maintain the Treasury Department is harassing them because of Internal Revenue Service probes into their eligibility for tax-exempt status. The Scientologists charge the Atomic Energy Commission with secrecy in its nuclear testing programs and with hiding evidence of radiation damage. They contend that the United States army uses brainwashing techniques and that the CIA practices mind control.

Scientology employs the Freedom of Information Act in its famous struggles against the FBI and the CIA, who, they charge, are illegally harassing them by keeping files on their members and by raiding and confiscating their property. Conflicts with the FBI date back to the 1950s. They maintain the FBI and CIA want to silence them because they expose dishonesty in the government and want to reform it.

In 1976 two Scientologists obtained jobs in the Internal Revenue Service and the Justice Department by using false credentials. They stole 15,000 documents from these offices relating to the church's tax-exempt status inquiries. On July 8, 1977, FBI agents raided Scientology headquarters in Los Angeles and Washington, D.C. The raids took over twenty hours and involved more than 165 FBI agents. They seized over 100,000 pages of documents to use as evidence against the church. The Scientologists filed a $7.5 million lawsuit against the FBI agents and two United States attorneys involved in the raids.

In August of 1978 eleven high Scientology officials, including Mary Sue Hubbard and the two men who had gained access to the IRS and Justice Department files, were indicted on twenty-eight counts including conspiracy to spy on United States agencies, breaking into government offices, stealing government documents, "bugging" federal agency meetings, and conspiracy to obstruct justice. Two of the defendants, Jane Kember, the church's director in England, and Morrison Budlong, "Deputy Guardian for Information Worldwide," are still in England fighting extradition to the United States.

A Federal Judge in Washington, D.C. declared the Washington FBI raid illegal and ordered the material seized from the headquarters there returned, but in September, 1979, the raid on the Los Angeles headquarters was declared legal and the 48,000 documents seized there permitted to be used for the government's case.

The trial was set to begin in September, 1979, but instead the defendants were permitted to submit a written plea of guilty to a single count of conspiracy to steal government documents while keeping the right to appeal the case. In lieu of a trial the government prepared a written record to support its case against the church. On October 26, Federal District Court Judge Charles R. Richey convicted eight of the defendants—Mary Sue Hubbard, Henning Heldt, Duke Snider, Gregory Willardson, Richard Weigland, Mitchell Hermann, Cindy Raymond, and Gerald Bennett Wolfe—on the single count of conspiracy to steal government documents and the ninth defendant, Sharon Thomas, of a misdemeanor theft count. In early December Judge Richey sentenced Hubbard, Raymond, and Wolfe each to five years in prison and a $10,000 fine. Heldt, Snider, Weigland, Willardson, and Hermann each received sentences of four years and a $10,000 fine, and Thomas was sentenced to six months and a $1,000 fine. Richey also ordered the ten-inch stack of documents seized in the government raids released to the public. In January, 1980, Judge Richey released the Scientologists from prison on bail, pending the appeal of their convictions.

The Scientologists' legal problems are not confined to the United States. In 1968, after receiving many complaints about the group, then Secretary for Health, Kenneth Robinson, conducted an investigation into their activities in England. He concluded that Scientology was a "socially harmful, pseudo-philosophical cult." The British government imposed a ban on the entry into England of all persons wishing to work for or study Scientology there. The church appealed the decision and in 1971 another inquiry was conducted. Attorney Sir John Foster recommended that the ban be lifted, but his proposal was not implemented. In February of 1979 Sir Idwal Pugh, the Parliamentary Commissioner (an Ombudsman of the Parliament), concluded the ban should be lifted. In an attempt to lobby support for ending the ban, Scientologists sent Pugh's report to over one hundred members of the British Parliament and in March petitioned Queen Elizabeth to intervene. They claim the ban on entry into the country of the movement's foreign students is a "discriminatory immigration restriction" that damages their civil rights, especially since the government has never made public the evidence from the inquiry which was the basis for the ban in 1968. In September of 1979 Baroness Edith von Thungen Reichenbach of Munich, Germany, was kept from entering the country when she challenged the ban. After the incident a British Home Office spokesman said the government's ban on Scientology was "under review."

The church has fought legal battles in Australia also. In 1965, the State of Victoria passed a Psychological Practices Act to regulate Scientology's practices and in 1968 Southern and Western Australia legislated to ban the church. However, according to Scientology sources, the restrictions have been ineffective. The only attempt to enforce the ban in Western Australia was made in 1969 when several Scientologists were fined. That decision was reversed by the Australian

Supreme Court, which "effectually ruled the ban invalid" according to the Scientologists. In 1973 the Australian Federal Attorney General authorized Scientology ministers to perform marriages. The Scientologists claim this was a great victory because the government thereby recognized Scientology as a religion and, in effect, negated the previous legislation attempting to ban it.

The church now faces additional legal problems in the United States. In June, 1979, the Scientologists were accused of fraudulently obtaining loans as high as $10,000 from California banks and finance companies and giving the money to the church. Law enforcement officials believe that Scientology leaders encouraged the church members to make false financial statements on the loan applications and then verified them. As many as one hundred Scientologists might be involved in the alleged scheme. Two have admitted in affidavits to obtaining the loans.

Chapter 3

THE TARGET IS YOU!
WHO JOINS AND WHY?

"Unbelievable!" "Incredible!" "Unreal!" That's how most people reacted to the mass suicides and murders at the People's Temple settlement in Guyana. In the most widely reported news event since the 1941 Japanese attack on Pearl Harbor—the Gallup Poll reported that 98 percent of all Americans heard about the Jonestown deaths—the question of the hour was "Why?" Why would so many apparently "normal" people, some wealthy and well educated, submit themselves to a tyrannical leader like Jim Jones? Why would they kill themselves and their small children on his orders?

Who Joins the Cults?

But as the shock and horror of the "Kool-Aid deaths" eased, public attention turned to another, more general set of questions. Who joins the cults? What kind of person is attracted to them? What is their appeal? Why are there so many cults on the world scene at this time? The sun-baked bodies in Guyana

97

sent a deep shudder through millions of people as they asked themselves, "Could someone in my family be susceptible to a cult? Am *I* a candidate for a cult?"

Hard data on cult membership is scarce. If accurate membership records are kept, the cults don't release them, and they do not make public any sociological data about their followers even if they do gather it. However, sociologists and psychologists are beginning to study cult members. Dr. Marc Galanter released a study in early 1979 in which he had interviewed 273 Unification Church members. Investigator Galen Kelly recently prepared a statistical analysis of cult members based on interviews of 100 people his firm has deprogrammed over a period of four years. Their findings confirm what cult observers have long believed—the cults have an almost identical target group in their search for new members.

Most cult members are between eighteen and twenty-six years of age. In his study Kelly found that 58 percent of the women and 41 percent of the men were eighteen to twenty years old when they joined the cult and 32 percent of the women and 53 percent of the men were twenty-one to twenty-five years old. Only 3 percent were seventeen years old or younger and 3 percent were above the age of twenty-six years. Eighteen is a significant age since it marks legal adulthood when many parental rights are ended or sharply limited.

Cult members are predominantly white. The Kelly study indicates that whites constitute 98 percent of cult membership, Blacks and other minorities 2 percent. Marc Galanter found that 89 percent of the Unification Church members he interviewed were white. The Reverend Jim Jones's People's Temple drew many Blacks, but it was an exception. One explanation is that Blacks and Hispanics, especially young people, are too "street smart" to join movements that promise instant happiness. As one Black teenager puts it: "For me its TCB (taking care of business). That comes first, putting bread on the table. I've no time for this bliss stuff. That's for rich white kids." Minority members generally do not have the leisure time and social mobility necessary to fall prey to the cults. It is the back-packing, guitar-in-hand wanderer that cult recruiters often approach. One frequently hears of Ivy League students recruited by the cults in Berkeley, California, or of Texas students joining a cult in Cambridge, Massachusetts. Cult recruiters have little success in getting either Black converts or cash contributions in Black neighborhoods.

Most cult members are single, at least when they enter the group. None of Kelly's former members had been married. Only 9 percent of Galanter's interviewees were married. There is a higher percentage of men than women in cult life, especially in such groups as Hare Krishna and Children of God where women are subservient to men. Galen Kelly found 62 percent of the cultists he had deprogrammed were men, 38 percent women.

Prospective cult members come primarily from middle-class and upper middle-class economic backgrounds. Kelly found 32 percent of the former members he surveyed came from families with incomes of $10,000 to $20,000 per year, 38 percent from families with incomes ranging from $21,000 to $35,000 per year and 30 percent from families with incomes of over $35,000 per year. No one came from families earning under $10,000 per year. The children of physicians, dentists, lawyers and "captains of industry" are overrepresented, and critics charge that the cults zero in on this group for recruitment since new converts can turn over trust funds, savings accounts, and family legacies.

It is, however, not merely wealthy young people who are sought out, but intelligent and industrious ones as well. Most cult members are well educated. Galen Kelly found 58 percent of the ex-cultists he had deprogrammed had some college education and 20 percent had completed college. Two percent had gone on for graduate work. Sixteen percent had completed high school only and 4 percent had less than a high-school education. Kelly's research indicates that 72 percent of his subjects were of average intelligence, 24 percent above average, and 4 percent "extraordinary." There were none classified as below average. Galanter also found that 58 percent of the Unification Church members he studied had been in college before joining the group, and one fourth had completed their studies. Dr. Thomas Ungerleider of the Department of Psychiatry at the UCLA Medical School studied a smaller number of Unification Church members than did Galanter but his 1979 survey also included IQ testing. Ungerleider reports his subjects registered higher than average scores.

If the cult member is recruited at college, the first and last years of undergraduate school seem to be the periods of most likely entry. The freshman year is usually the first time a young man or woman leaves home for an extended period of time and it is often filled with troubling personal adjustments. The faculty members may be figures who have little real contact with their freshmen students, and many times the student has no meaningful communication with any adult. The college freshman is rebelling against his parents and finds the new alternatives in sex, politics, and religion attractive. The young freshman is also struggling with himself: he wants independence, yet at the same time fears it.

The senior year, especially the last semester, is also a crucial time, as he is about to leave the comfort and routine of undergraduate life. Friends, roommates, and the familiar paths will soon be left behind as the student ends a four-year period of growth and development. For the first time he must face an uncertain future in the "real world" where admission to graduate school is highly competitive and the job market is shrinking. The anxiety of entering a new phase of life can be extreme. Cults such as the Divine Light Mission, Hare Krishna, the Unification Church, and the Children of God offer the possibility of a new "cocoon," a new extended family which promises absolute security in a highly alien and competitive world. Many students have actually joined a cult within four weeks of their college graduation when a kind of panic overwhelms them.

The Religious Background of Cultists

What are the religious backgrounds of cult members? Here, too, accurate statistics are hard to come by and often vary. Father James Le Bar, Communications Officer of the Roman Catholic Archdiocese of New York, estimates that about 45 percent of Unification Church members are from a Roman Catholic background, 40 percent from Protestant families, and 10 to 12 percent from Jewish families. Galen Kelly found that 40 percent of his deprogrammed subjects were Protestant, 30 percent Catholic, and 30 percent Jewish. Some observers believe as many as 50 percent of Unification Church members may be Jewish. Since the Jewish community is less than 3 percent of the total American population, even Le Bar's figure of 10 to 12 percent is a cause for deep concern among Jews.

Observers estimate that perhaps 20 percent of Hare Krishnas are Jewish. Jews constitute as much as 30 percent of Divine Light Mission membership and there are many Jews in Scientology. The Way International, The Alamo Foundation, and the Children of God draw more Christians.

One Catholic who did not want her name revealed gives a possible explanation for the high percentage of Roman Catholics in cults:

> I was raised in the post-Vatican Council church, but I heard my parents and grandparents reminisce about the way it used to be when there was no meat on Friday, strictly Latin masses, novenas, everyone went to Confession . . . I never knew that kind of Catholic church and I yearned for strict authority and discipline. Since I couldn't find it in today's church, I found it elsewhere, in a cult.

Dr. J. Stillson Judah, Professor Emeritus of the Pacific School of Religion, surveyed Unification Church members in 1977 and concluded that most followers did not consider themselves members of their parents' religious community at the time they joined the Unification Church. "Although a good percentage were Jewish, only 1 percent listed Judaism as their spiritual search," Judah explains. He found that only 3.5 percent considered themselves strong or active Christians before joining the Moon organization.

But it is an oversimplification to conclude that only those with weak training or background in their own religion join the cults. Many come from strong Catholic or Evangelical Christian backgrounds and there are some cult members who received intensive Orthodox Jewish upbringings, including attendance in Jewish day schools.

How reliable are these statistics on cult membership? Galanter and Ungerleider studied only the Unification Church and Kelly surveyed only former cult members. However, Kelly points out that the cases he studied are "more representative than they would initially appear" as the study covers a four-year period of time and the subjects were geographically distributed throughout the United States. It is interesting to note that in most instances the statistics in the Galanter and Kelly surveys parallel each other closely. More studies involving a larger number of people, more variety of cults, and both those still in and those who have left the groups are needed.

The available statistics should not lead to stereotyping of cult members. It is a mistake, for example, to believe that only college students are attracted to the cults. As the Galanter and Kelly studies indicate, about 40 percent did not attend college prior to their cult experience. There are many followers who have abandoned jobs rather than schooling to join a cult and others who retain their jobs but give most of their money and leisure time to these groups. It is also an error to believe that only the young are in cults. There are middle-aged and even older followers as well. Some who entered a cult when they were young have matured within it, married, and had children now being raised in the cult. Often, as in the Jonestown settlement, entire family units may be involved. Part of the tragedy of the cult phenomenon is the breakup of families if some members leave and others stay in the group. There are many sad tales of parents who have children remaining in the cults which they have left, usually with the other parent, and some ex-cultists are battling to regain legal custody of their small children.

Is There a Typical Cult Member?

Is there a psychological profile that fits the "typical" cult convert? Are there some psychological traits, similar behavior patterns, or family histories that can help predict suscepti- bility to cults? At a recent meeting of psychologists and psy- chiatrists one therapist rose and announced he had discovered the "prime cult type": "It is an eighteen-year-old with an undifferentiated personality, one that is not yet formed or matured." A colleague quickly responded: "Show me most eighteen-year-olds and I'll show you an undifferentiated per- sonality!" The other participants laughed as they nodded their heads, agreeing that few teenagers' personalities are firmly established.

The story illustrates that it is not easy to discern a consis- tent personality pattern in cult members. It is too facile to ascribe psychological disorders or dead or absent parents as the causes of cult membership. Comments Dr. Margaret Singer, a psychiatrist on the staff of the Wright Institute at Berkeley, California, and the University of California in San Francisco who has counseled more than four hundred cult members:

> Almost anyone who is lonely and in between meaningful attach- ments is in a vulnerable period in which he or she might get taken in by the flattery and deception lures that the cults use to recruit new members. There is no single type of person, but a wide range of individuals who become involved with cults.

No single element brings a person into a cult, and as Dr. Singer suggests, "Simply being depressed may not be quite sufficient, or being in between commitments may not be enough, but the combination of being in between jobs, in between romances, in between college and a first job, and *also* depressed would certainly make the person extremely vulnerable." Dr. George Swope, an American Baptist minister, is a faculty member at a community college in Westchester County, New York, and a psychologist who has had extensive experience with former cult members. He agrees that no family is immune: "Cult members are no different from anyone else. Given the right time, place, and circumstances, anyone is vulnerable," he says.

Galanter and Kelly attempted to study past life experiences and emotional problems and family environment prior to cult involvement. Galanter found that many of his subjects joined the Unification Church in a period of personal crisis; two thirds of the 237 men and women admitted they had experienced emotional or drug-related problems before joining. Of those who admitted to emotional distress, one third had previously sought professional help and 6 percent had been hospitalized. Kelly found that 30 percent of those he studied had regularly used hard drugs before they joined a cult and 60 percent admitted to "light or occasional use of various drugs." Eight percent made "heavy use of hard drugs" and 3 percent classified themselves as drug addicts. Only 2 percent reported no drug usage prior to joining a cult. Four percent reported chronic physical ailments or serious medical history. Two percent had been in trouble with the law. When Kelly questioned them as to their emotional stability, 68 percent reported "mild adolescent difficulties," 20 percent "serious difficulties," and 12 percent were classified as "psychotic/borderline psychotic." None were listed as "highly stable." Kelly also tried to analyze the emotional stability of their families. Only 4 percent listed their families as highly stable, 52 percent reported "minor difficulties," 34 percent "serious difficulties," and 10 percent "psychotic/borderline psychotic" family situations.

Although more studies of this type are needed and one cannot generalize, these figures do show that a high percentage of cult members experienced emotional turmoil before joining a

cult. Kelly did not attempt to analyze whether cult membership helped to solve these problems, but Galanter found that
Unification Church membership seemed to stabilize the earlier psychological problems and distress. Galanter also studied
119 Divine Light Mission members and found a similar sharp
decline in neurotic symptoms among those followers.

Since the Unification Church's cooperation was necessary in
the Galanter study it is quite possible that the interviewees
were preselected by the church and only the most "well-
adjusted" followers were presented for interviews. Nonetheless, this survey is a useful first step towards gaining data
about the effects of cult membership.

Why Are Cults So Attractive Now?

There have always been people with emotional problems or
problems with their families, and there have always been
vulnerable people alone and adrift in life, between jobs,
schools, and romances. Why are the cults so successful in
attracting members now? One answer to that important question lies in the attitudes many men and women have about our
society.

The grand hopes of science—its promises and claims and
even its highly regarded "objective method"—have under-
gone severe challenges in the 1970s. Critics of science point to
the nuclear radiation at Three Mile Island, the defective
DC-10 airplanes, the crashing Skylab, toxic wastes in the
ground, air and water pollution, and the high incidence of
cancer apparently caused by environmental factors. Some
people want to "drop out" of our technology-gone-wild world.
This sense of disenchantment and disillusionment is prevalent
in many converts to the cults. A world apparently out of control with scientific "mistakes" everywhere makes the absolute claims of the cults an attractive alternative to the obvious
colossal errors of our contemporary society.

Present in almost all cult converts is the pervasive feeling
that every major institution in our lives is discredited and

unworthy of support. Not only is the scientific community widely distrusted, but so too is the military establishment, big business, big labor, academic institutions, the family, all government, and the traditional organized religions. While there have always been young people who were wary or distrustful of the "establishment," today's cult members are more intense and embittered than others in their contempt for Western society. In the past, the "system" was able to absorb or coopt its critics. The eighteen- to twenty-six-year-old age group accepted the flaws of the system but compromised to work within it by going on to graduate school, entering military service, marrying early and having children, voting in elections and going into entry-level positions in government or the private sector. But today the high rate of unemployment and galloping inflation, the fierce competition for graduate school places and the uncertainty of the quality of the future make participation in the system more difficult. By joining the cults they choose a different path.

Today, more than ever, people search for meaning and purpose in life. They realize that material goods and the pursuit of pleasure have not brought happiness. People ask, in the words of the song made famous by Peggy Lee, "Is That All There Is?" At this point the cults appear on the scene offering singleness of purpose. In a decadent society they preach a radiant, transcendent ideal, a meaningful way of life that is not merely a continuation of consumerism and conspicuous consumption. "No, that's not all there is," declares the cult recruiter. "Our group offers meaning in life, goals to aim for, and a purpose to existence."

A. C. Bhaktivedanta Swami Prabhupada explains that his Hare Krishna movement has been so successful in the West

because your materialistic way of life no longer satisfies them [people]. In America, especially, you have got enough for enjoyment. You have got enough food, enough women, enough wine, enough houses . . . But still you have confusion and dissatisfaction . . . So it is necessary now that people should take to spiri-

tual life. That will make them happy. All these people—they are
in darkness . . . But when you are spiritually situated you know
what you are doing and where you are going. Everything is
clear.*

Swami Prabhupada lays part of the blame for the rampant
"confusion and dissatisfaction" at the door of Western religion. It has failed, he believes, because Western religious
leaders "are not really interested in religion. It is simply show-
bottle. If you do not follow the regulative principles, then
where is your religion?"

Indeed, mainstream Western religion no longer seems to be
satisfying to many today. Statistics bear this out. From 1965
to 1975, seven of the ten largest Christian denominations lost
an average of 10 percent of their members and baptisms and
church-school enrollments plummeted. There were sharp de-
clines also in the numbers of Roman Catholics attending
Mass. As their church has tried to modernize itself, it has lost
members. Similarly, the rapid growth rate of the 1950s and
1960s of Judaism's Reform movement has come to an end,
and many Jews are either turning away from their religion or
turning toward the more emotional and rigorous Orthodox
branch. *The New York Times* reported in October of 1979 that
a recent Gallup poll indicated that 41 percent of adult Americans—61 million people—classify themselves as "unchurched"
even though they hold traditional religious beliefs. According
to a recent Gallup Associated Press Youth Survey only one
fourth of America's teenagers "express a high degree of confidence in organized religion" although one third of them de-
scribe themselves as "very religious" and 95 percent say they
believe in God. The overwhelming emotional reception given
to Pope John Paul II—by non-Catholics as well as Catholics—
during his visits to Ireland and the United States in the

---

*"Rascals, Bluffers and Show-Bottle Spiritualists." From an interview with his
Divine Grace A. C. Bhaktivedanta Swami Prabhupada in *Back to Godhead*
(Los Angeles: Bhaktivedanta Book Trust, 1979), p.3.

autumn of 1979 illustrated the spiritual hunger many feel. Cult members cite another fault with our society—there are no more heroes or heroines, no authentic role models on the public scene. Heroes such as John Kennedy, Martin Luther King, Jr., and Robert Kennedy were snatched from us. Richard Nixon brought disgrace to the American Presidency. Everyone, especially young people, needs a role model and the prospective cult member sees none and may look elsewhere and find his hero or role model in a cult leader.

Cults are attractive today also because of political fatigue and frustration, a feeling of helplessness and of being powerless to effect changes through political processes. In the 1960s there was also widespread disenchantment with the perceived inequalities in America, and some of the youth leaders developed a comprehensive radical critique that included alleged American war crimes committed in Vietnam, institutionalized racism, and anti-student policies in many college and university administrations. The remedy for these evils was also a radical, active one: rapid change, immediate abolition of all unfair practices and policies, replacement of antiquated and unjust laws, participatory democracy, and "power to the people."

Today the critique remains much the same, but it is now set against yet another decade of unmet needs, unfulfilled promises, and a worsening economic and energy crisis throughout the world. Although there are still those who offer a radical solution to today's conditions they are few in number and lack the widespread support of the earlier leaders. But the cults, not strong a decade ago, offer a new—yet really very old— solution to the problems. Cult leaders and adherents agree with the 1960s critique of society, but instead of proposing a radical solution, one that would offer increased freedom to individuals, more personal choices, a greater role in society's decision-making processes, a greater sharing of the world's natural resources (all 1960s themes), the cults present a backward-looking cure. As Robert J. Lifton, author of *Thought Reform and the Psychology of Totalism,* explains, "The cults make a radical critique of society but the solutions they offer are reactionary." They call for abdication of self in favor of the group's aims. They offer the exalted goal of personal salvation, but with the surrender of one's personal freedom and individual choice as the price. Many people for whom the political struggle is simply too burdensome retreat from freedom into the waiting arms of a cult that offers a total and perfect solution to an unsatisfying and imperfect world. This willingness to surrender is the most significant difference between today's youth and those of a decade ago. One generation chose the expansion of human freedom and personal liberty, and the other generation enters the cults and yields those freedoms willingly.

Cults are attracting members not only because of the perceived evils and flaws of society but also because of inner drives and feelings of potential converts.

Today's students have more time for personal reflection. No longer do they put their energies into social or campus reform. The campus is relatively stable. Gone are the barricades, the personal insecurity caused by the military draft, the horrors of the Vietnam War, the scandal of Watergate, and the lure of the political "New Left."

Young people, and their elders as well, are showing less concern for the welfare of others and are turning inward. Ours is an age of privatism, when our basic commitments have shifted from concern about the general society and its well-being to concern about ourselves. Our ultimate interests and loyalties are limited solely to "Numero Uno." Journalist Tom Wolfe has dubbed the seventies the "Me Generation." Many people are trying to tune in on their inner spiritual lives through psychological therapies such as EST and exploration of the occult through such things as witchcraft, "pyramid power," out-of-body experiences, and ESP.

People are seeking a deeply personal and emotional religious experience, one not based upon the traditional Christian and Jewish disciplines of rigorous study, slow spiritual growth, and an abiding commitment to the principles of social justice.

The profound intellectual demands of Moses Maimonides, Thomas Acquinas, or Reinhold Niebuhr have been replaced by the frenzied search for a "quick fix" in religion, a high-intensity immediate experience. There is an impatience, a demand for "instant answers" to the unanswerable metaphysical questions that have always vexed humanity.

This intense spiritual search is accompanied by a disturbing anti-intellectualism. Some of the cults denounce the kind of knowledge gained at schools as "satanic," "corrupt," and "impure," and even claim it stands in the way to spiritual fulfillment. Only the cult can offer "perfect knowledge," and that perfection stems not from the intellectual processes of traditional religion but from the immediate, experiential encounter with the cult and its leader.

Yet today's calm campus is the scene of increased interest in religion. During the past five years a large number of schools have reported surging enrollments in religious studies. Ithaca College in New York State, for example, has added twenty-three new courses in religion since 1974. Attendance at worship services is climbing. "More and more students are delighted to discover that the act of worship can be enjoyable," observed Father Ambrose McInnis, director of Tulane University's Catholic Center. There are four different Jewish Sabbath services conducted at the University of Pennsylvania, all well attended. Students had to be turned away from the 1979 Jewish High Holy Day services at Harvard because they couldn't be accommodated.

It was not always so. In the 1950s and 1960s science and its claims reigned almost unchallenged on America's campuses and those who professed a traditional belief in religion were pleasantly tolerated at best or sharply derided at worst by fellow students and faculty members. A former Wesleyan student of the 1950s remembers:

The big question then was, Does God conform to the scientific method? Unless you had a God concept that satisfied that method you were looked upon as some kind of benighted holdover from the Middle Ages. I was religious at Wesleyan, but I hid it from many of my friends. I guess I was a closet believer.

Today, however, the "big questions" on the campus are quite different: "What kind of head trip are you into? What kind of meditation method do you use? Which guru do you follow?" The cults feed upon such questions and offer an alternative that is both anti-intellectual and a retreat from the uncomfortable ambiguity, skepticism, and cynicism of the modern age in which the validity of absolutes is denied and everything is nuanced and delicately balanced. Daily life is filled with such qualifying phrases as "on the other hand." Yeats warned that when "the best lack all conviction the worst are full of passionate intensity." Theodore Roszak, Professor of History at California State University at Hayward and a keen observer of the culture of contemporary American youth, believes that in such a time as ours, "The quacks and rascals are free to announce the futility of intellect and to appeal to blind faith and gut feeling." Bewildered, frightened, unnerved by the world as it is, the potential cult member, in desperation, makes a total surrender, a fanatical commitment to the cult in the hope of overcoming the uncertainties of life.

This surrender to absolute authority which relieves the cult member of agonizing large decisions and even sometimes of small, day-to-day decisions is an abdication of freedom and personal liberty in favor of security. It is an ominous trend wherever cults are successful. A significant and growing number have turned their backs on our society and have opted instead for a closed system of belief, work, and friendship, but the price paid for such security is a high one.

Just as attractive as the security of submission to the guidance of an absolute authority is the appeal of disciplined personal sacrifice that the cults demand. Professor Harvey Cox of the Harvard Divinity School reminds us that we often underestimate the power and attractiveness of sacrifice, particularly among young people.

A generation of middle- and upper middle-class young

people has grown up in physical affluence, and the need to sacrifice some of that wealth and privilege, about which there is often deep guilt, may be overwhelming. Ours is a society that makes few demands upon its members. Conventional religions ask little from their believers—the notable exceptions are Evangelical Christianity and Orthodox Judaism, and it is not surprising that both of these groups are growing rapidly. In such a milieu a cult leader who demands personal sacrifices of money, time, talent, energy, and as we saw in Jonestown, even life itself will find thousands of receptive converts waiting only to be told what to give up or surrender for a promised greater good. If the general society and established religious groups either neglect or spurn this urge to give, that powerful drive will be satisfied elsewhere. That is why many cult members joyously transfer their savings accounts to a cult, why they deliberately lead a rigid, spartan life of self-denial while they are in the group, and why so many are willing to work long hours in often humiliating jobs, all enthusiastically done in the name of sacrifice.

As part of that sacrifice the followers in many cults live a life of "white-knuckled puritanism." A strict regimen is part of the price paid to earn the leader's "unconditional" love. In the quest for absolute purity and in the spirit of self-sacrifice the young man or woman may give up drugs, alcohol, smoking, and all sexual activity. Some women in the cults have ceased menstruating for months and even years; young men have stopped growing facial hair. Many report that they are so exhausted and malnourished that they lose their sexual drive altogether.

This sexual repression is appealing to members who, before joining the group, experienced difficulty handling the increased sexual freedom of today. One major attraction of the cults is that they remove the necessity of coping with sexual freedom and responsibility. All sexual concerns are taken care of in the name of religious purity. The prohibition of drugs also gives comforting specific limits to many members who previously had none. Parents of cult members are often at first pleased to learn of these restrictions, but in time are confronted with a difficult choice: Should their children continue their sexual adventures and drug usage outside of the cult or join an authoritarian group and pay the price for these limits? Some parents may at first be thankful that their children appear to have "found themselves" but soon realize that the repression of normal sexual drives, the withdrawal from the outside world, the narrow focus of interests and activities and even the cult member's limited vocabulary are signs that he has given up on the "impure" world and his old life. It signals not only sacrifice but also a total capitulation to the values and norms of the cult.

Women may find the cults attractive because they no longer have to deal with the new choices available to them as a result of the women's liberation movement. It is ironic that in an age of new sexual freedom and expanded career opportunities so many women choose the cult life's severe restrictions.

The strong appeal of the cults, especially to young people, can also be explained by the power of peer pressure. The prospective cult member often wavers just before making a commitment to the group, perhaps asking himself, "Should I join this community of love, friendship and solidarity, or should I return to my school, family, friends, and job?" Poised on a delicate fulcrum, he can go either way. Often the force that tips someone toward cult membership is peer pressure, and so the cult may use peers to exert strong persuasion at that critical point. The potential member's ego is "stroked" continuously from all sides by followers to make him feel important. The attractive promise of pulling together, of joining others to make a difference in a sinful and corrupt world, can be a key factor. There are countless reports of wavering candidates being pulled into a small room and "love-bombed" with great intensity by peers in the cult. The carefully orchestrated "love bombing" is manipulative and yet touches something quite deep in human existence. Who among us does not like to hear others mention our name again and again? Who among us does not enjoy the pleasure of having others take our words and opinions seriously? Since childhood we have been thrilled at being part of the "in group," and not being "odd man out."

Exceedingly high parental expectations often cause young people to join a cult. Parents usually define their hope for their children's "success" according to materialistic values. The intense pressure to achieve, to excel, to be successful, is sometimes overwhelming. The child may fear that he or she can never reach the high goals set for him by his parents, and, rather than disappoint them, may instead totally reject the success goal and simply refuse to compete in the arenas of the business or professional world. The cults offer a secure world seemingly free of personal competition, academic grades, and status based upon financial income or profession. For years some parents have asked their children, "What do you want to be when you grow up? A doctor, lawyer, industrialist?" Membership in a cult is one way a child answers that question.

Cults Provide a Caring Community

But the main reason people join cults is as old as humanity itself: the search for a caring community. Perhaps the root cause of the cult appeal is the loneliness and alienation that many men and women of all ages experience. The cries and whispers of the alienated are all around us, as can be seen in the abysmally low percentage of eligible voters who cast ballots, the rapid spread of a myriad of self-help groups, the sharp increase in liquor consumption among the young, the continuing high rate of drug usage, and the accelerating divorce rate. Widespread alienation is the soil in which the cults flourish.

A major symptom of this intense loneliness and despair is the rising suicide rate, especially among young people. Medical specialists and college officials consider suicide to be one of the major challenges now facing American society. According to a 1979 Public Affairs Committee of New York City study about four hundred thousand young people attempt to commit suicide annually, and more than four thousand suceed.

The committee's research indicates that fifteen- to twenty-four-year-olds are especially susceptible to suicide because they are going through a period of intense inner turmoil, confusion, and search for personal identity, and are often subject to deep feelings of helplessness and hopelessness. Suicides of young people occur in all economic groups, from all levels of education and from every social class and religious, ethnic, and racial background. Ironically, the suicide rate among college students has dramatically increased even as the campuses have outwardly calmed down after the turbulence of the 1960s.

The siren song of the cults is simple and profound: "We love you. We are a family. We care about you. Join our community and share in this bliss and love." For many, it is "an offer they cannot refuse." As former Unification Church member Christopher Edwards explains in *Crazy for God:*

> I desperately hoped that, if there was a God of love, there were others like myself with whom I could share my desires. Perhaps somewhere out there was a community where I would be free to love and learn and where I would be loved and taught, as I had wanted so much at college and so sadly missed.

Edwards relates that this search for community overpowered even his realization that the Unification Church lectures were not convincing intellectually.

> Garbage [the lectures], I thought. Yet I longed so deeply for Community . . . I desired so much to realize my hopes and goals in a communal framework . . . I wanted so badly to believe.

Clearly, it is this yearning to belong to a community of love that is at the heart of the cultic appeal. Traditionally, families and religions have provided us with our deepest feelings of identity and belonging to a shared community. The *raison d'être* of both Judaism and Christianity has always been to provide their followers membership in the "people of God." Jews regard themselves as an extended family and try to live by the concept that they are interdependent and responsible one to another. Christians are "brothers and sisters in Christ," members of the Church Universal. Both religions stress the joy of belonging to a spiritual, caring, and loving community. But this message is apparently not getting through to many people. Explains Dr. Barbara Hargrove, a sociologist of religion at the Iliff School of Theology in Denver, Colorado:

> The experience of a bounded moral community is missing. We ask these young people to ask questions but we give them nothing to ask questions about. We give them no identity in the moral context. Society has created a generation of religious illiterates.

In the absence of satisfying and authentic communities within traditional religion, people will seek it elsewhere. The new religious cults have successfully met this need by establishing meeting houses, communes, retreat centers, and farms, all communities of concern. It is no accident that the Unification Church calls itself "The Family" and The Church of Armageddon is known as "The Love Family." Not only is one a member of a strong community of love in these cults, but a member of a unique, elite, elect, chosen one that is armed with a special knowledge. One may be a member of a community that believes it is the "righteous remnant" that will survive the end of time to begin the world anew. The cult recruit becomes an important member of the ultimate "in group," one that will transcend the destruction of the evil world and be the architect of the new order.

Although it is difficult to generalize, it appears that the most vulnerable target group for cult recruitment is the person, young or old, who has made no meaningful connection with an established religion, who is in search of spiritual values and transcendent meaning, who is willing, even yearning for strict discipline and authority, and who may be burdened with guilt about affluence or sex or drugs. Such a person may enthusiastically make the sacrifices necessary to maintain the love of the cult leader and of his peers within the group. In an age of dislocation, when everything and everyone seems rootless and in flux, when one's own family is seen as superficial and vapid, one's own religion as irrelevant and relativistic, and society as chaotic and uncaring, the absolute claims, guarantees, and promises of cult life are appealing.

Chapter 4

COUNTERING
THE CULTS

When Representative Leo Ryan of California, along with three members of the press who accompanied him to Guyana in November, 1978, was murdered by members of the People's Temple, he was attempting to provide a legal and safe means for the cult's members to leave it. Ryan's goal has yet to be achieved, and today it is the major concern for parents of cult members and for many religious, medical, legal, and public officials as well.

Legal Options for Parents

Parents are increasingly turning to the law courts for assistance after earlier attempts to extricate their children by reasoning, pleading, and even physical force have failed. Believing their children victims of psychological coercion, duplicity, and kidnaping, they are going to court to reclaim them. Two main legal remedies are open to parents, but both are highly problematic.

One legal option is for parents to become court-appointed conservators or guardians of their cultist children who are over the legal age of eighteen. Under the law, most parental rights end at eighteen, but in conservatorship cases, parents attempt to regain legal control of their children, in effect becoming responsible for their welfare. The original intent of the conservatorship laws was to protect the aged, senile, and/or infirm from being victimized by unscrupulous confidence men who often tricked them out of their money and property. In such cases either the state or the adult child of the victim became the legal guardian of the one who was unable to protect himself. Now this same law is being applied to cases of alleged psychological coercion and mind alteration as parents seek legal control of their children.

Some parents hesitate to use this legal strategy because guardianship or conservatorship is granted only when the court feels the child is legally incompetent and such a ruling becomes a matter of public record. Even when confronted with their child's cult membership, some parents do not want the ruling to be public knowledge.

Professor Alan W. Scheflin of the University of Santa Clara Law School and a coauthor of the book, *The Mind Manipulators,* feels that the judges have been willing to consider the charge of psychological coercion even though it is difficult to prove legally. Jeremiah S. Gutman, Chairman of the American Civil Liberty Union's Privacy Committee and an attorney who has represented cult members in such cases, rejects the psychological coercion charge: "If a parent is distraught, that's too bad. That's what the First Amendment is about. Adults can choose friends even if papa doesn't like them."

In the best known conservatorship case, in March, 1977, California State Superior Court Judge S. Lee Vavuris placed five Unification Church members in the temporary custody of their parents. The parents claimed their children, ranging in age from twenty-one to twenty-six, were "brainwashed" and needed to leave Moon's church to regain "normalcy." Judge

Vavuris ruled: "We are talking about the essence of civilization—mother, father, and children . . . I know of no greater love than parents for their children . . . The child is the child even though the parent may be ninety and the child sixty." Judge Vavuris's verdict was quickly overturned by a higher state court, but four of the five young people did not return to the Unification Church following deprogramming. However, because of this case there are currently no legal efforts in California to regain children by the conservatorship process.

Some cult members, probably at the instigation of and with the financial backing of their cult, have contested their parents' attempt to gain guardianship status over them. They claim they are content in the cult and have gained spiritual satisfaction. In May, 1977, Donna Seidenberg Bavis sued an attorney, a county judge, and deprogrammers for $500,000, claiming they violated her constitutional rights by granting her mother a guardianship decree. The case is still pending in the United States District Court of Maryland.

A second legal tactic parents are pursuing is to obtain a *habeas corpus* writ to remove a person from a cult. Generally, such writs have been directed at the state rather than at individuals or groups. However, if parents believe there is evidence a child is being held in a cult illegally or if a child's civil rights are being violated in any other way, a judge may issue a writ. The cult is then forced to bring the member in person before the court (*habeas corpus* is the Latin for "you shall produce a body"). The cult must show cause that the charges are baseless and without merit. As in conservatorship cases, cult members sometimes testify they are not being held in the group against their will and their civil rights are being fully exercised. *Habeas corpus* is a difficult procedure and the results have not been promising.

In 1978, Carolyn and Elton Helander attempted to direct a writ of *habeas corpus* against an individual, Neil Salonen, the president of the Unification Church in America in order to secure the release of their daughter, Wendy, from the group.

During the trial the Unification Church refused to produce Wendy in court, submitting instead a tape recording of her voice on which she insisted she had voluntarily joined the church. The District of Columbia Superior Court judge ruled against the parents, claiming that there was no evidence that the Unification Church was holding Wendy against her will. Wendy Helander is now suing deprogrammers and an anticult parental group for $9 million, charging them with unlawful imprisonment during her unsuccessful deprogramming.

In a similar case, in February, 1979, a New York State Supreme Court Justice ruled that the father of Barbara Anne Larson had failed to prove that the Unification Church was holding her against her will.

Deprogramming

By far the most effective means of getting people out of the cults has been deprogramming, a method pioneered in 1971 by Ted Patrick. A former Community Relations Aide to Governor Ronald Reagan in California, Patrick became concerned about religious cults after his son was approached by the Children of God. The term originated among cult critics after they observed the trancelike state of many cult followers and concluded they had been "programmed" by the cult, just as a computer is programmed with data by its operator. The deprogramming technique consists of asking probing questions to shake the cult member's beliefs and then confronting him with the duplicity and contradictions of the cult's doctrines. Parents and deprogrammers hope that through this confrontation process the follower will realize that he has been misled, abused, and manipulated by the cult and will leave it. Ted Patrick explains his method:

> Deprogramming is just simply telling the truth, getting a person's mind to working again . . . Once we get the mind open for the first time in so many days, weeks, months, or years, they

have something to compare with. When they start comparing, they start evaluating. When they start evaluating, they start thinking.

Barbara and Linda Fabe of Cincinnati, Ohio, both in their early twenties, were deprogrammed by Ted Patrick from the Divine Light Mission in late 1978. Barbara's account illustrates how the process works:

> The more they [the deprogrammers] talked, the more I became clearer and understood more and more. "Wait a minute, I'm not getting what I was promised . . . I'm not serving God . . ." I was one of the highest people . . . I have been very close with a lot of initiators who are the closest ones to Guru Maharaj Ji. And they didn't have it [enlightenment or spiritual certainty] and I don't have it, and I don't know anyone who has it.

To achieve this goal, deprogrammers need an uninterrupted period of time with the cult member away from any influence or contact with the cult and away from other distractions; ex-cult members are also needed to assist in the delicate, and emotionally charged deprogramming sessions. Just as former alcoholics and drug addicts are effective in helping others change their habits, so also former cult members are indispensable to any successful deprogramming effort.

Cults fight deprogrammers in every possible way. They teach their followers that it is a cross between the cruelty of the Spanish Inquisition and the modern secret police, and warn their followers that deprogrammers forcibly abduct them, lock them up, beat them, abuse and even starve them until they give in and renounce the cult. They circulate stories of brutal deprogrammings lasting for weeks. Ted Patrick is called "Black Lightning" by the cults, more because they fear him than because of his race. Cults are now suing many deprogrammers, claiming they are violating the cultists' civil rights.

Deprogramming seems to work. Patrick claims he has deprogrammed over sixteen hundred people, and only thirty have returned to the cults. Other deprogrammers cite similar success. Of the one hundred thirty cult members Galen Kelly has deprogrammed, twelve have been unsuccessful. But only one of these twelve, he explains, went back to the cult out of real conviction—the others went back because of "operational problems" such as bad security.

Studies conducted by Drs. Thomas Ungerleider and David Wallisch of UCLA's Department of Psychiatry indicate that the length of cult membership determines the success of deprogramming. Followers who belonged to a group for over a year are more likely to return to the cult after the deprogramming while those who were in for less than a year generally do not go back.

Former cult members Allen Tate Wood, Steve Hassan, Chrisopher Edwards, Paul Engle, Barbara Underwood (one of the "California Five"), and David Adler all have lectured and written extensively about their own successful deprogrammings. Hundreds of other former cult members insist they never would have left the cult on their own, that they came out only because of the deprogramming. Many of those deprogrammed speak eloquently of being "saved," "given another chance," "given a new life." Tom Fuller, who was in the Unification Church, recounts:

> I was given a chance to question whether this man whose picture I had been bowing down to twice a day was, in fact, the Messiah. The deprogramming was a gentle, loving experience which opened up the possibility of my beginning to think for myself again.

Margaret Singer believes those cult members who have been deprogrammed "get going faster and rejoin society. They're mad at first, but they soon appreciate being told the truth about the group." Those who leave the cults voluntarily—and they are far fewer in number than those who are deprogrammed—have a more difficult time reentering society, according to Dr. Singer.

Some believe deprogramming is the only way to counteract the psychological coercion practiced by some of the cults. The deprogramming process reverses the method used in coercive persuasion, they maintain, and is hence the only way to undo the damage. The few who do leave the cults without being deprogrammed experience psychological problems more acutely and "float" back more frequently and for longer periods of time into the trancelike state which they were in during cult life than do those who have gone through the deprogramming process. Flo Conway believes deprogramming is "the only remedy currently available for treating the states of mind produced by this cult experience." She believes it "should be recognized as a new and valuable form of mental-health therapy."

However, some counsel caution in the use of deprogramming. Psychologist Moshe Spero warns there can be some degree of psychiatric risk "specifically in cases involving individuals with weak personalities or with just below surface latent psychopathology *prior* to cult commitment." Others advise that there are untrained deprogrammers and some who are in it only for the money. Unskilled deprogrammers and those who charge highly inflated fees should be avoided.

Is Deprogramming Legal?

Ted Patrick has served jail sentences because his physical removal of members from a cult in order to deprogram them was ruled kidnaping. He is a defendant in several lawsuits brought by cult members such as that instigated by Wendy Helander. Other deprogrammers have paid heavy fines. In discussing the legality of deprogramming it is important to separate it from kidnaping, which is an illegal act. Cult members can often be persuaded to leave the group temporarily to talk to deprogrammers; a person can be deprogrammed without being forcibly removed from the cult.

Today many deprogrammers will not talk to a cult member unless he comes to the session willingly. However, in most deprogrammings some physical coercion is involved such as locking the cult member inside the premises.

In June, 1979, the United States Supreme Court refused to consider an appeal by Leslie Weiss, a Unification Church member who charged that Ted Patrick and Albert Turner had illegally attempted to deprogram her in 1974. Without commenting the Supreme Court let stand a December, 1978, ruling of the United States Circuit Court of appeals in Boston. That ruling affirmed a lower court ruling by Judge Francis J. Boyle of Providence that dismissed Ms. Weiss's complaint on the ground there was no evidence to indicate she had been held against her will. In her charges, Ms. Weiss said she had remained overnight at Mr. Turner's house and had "played along" with Patrick and Turner by making them believe she was being successfully deprogrammed. She later returned to the Unification Church.

Judge Boyle ruled that the two deprogrammers were motivated by the "solicitude" of Ms. Weiss's mother who feared that her daughter's psychological and physical health was being threatened by the church and not by animosity toward the group itself. He held that Patrick and Turner did not violate the federal civil rights act and were exercising their right of free speech in attempting to persuade Ms. Weiss to leave the cult. Because of the Supreme Court's refusal to review the case, Turner has urged other parents of cult members to attempt deprogramming as a means of removing them from the cults. The issue of deprogramming will probably reach the Supreme Court again in the future.

Since it is difficult, at best, to remove people from the cults, many wish to direct their efforts toward countering the cults and their activities. Public concern increased after the November, 1978, deaths in Guyana, and critics, parents, and public officials are currently studying existing criminal and civil laws to see whether they are applicable to the cults and their activities and are calling for more vigorous enforcement of these laws. They are also examining the possibility of enacting new legislation where appropriate to curb the cults' abuses.

First Amendment Issues

There are those who are hesitant to prosecute the new religious cults. At the heart of the issue is the First Amendment of the United States Constitution which historically has protected unconventional, unpopular, and exotic religious groups. While those parents and other critics who urge more vigorous legal scrutiny of the cults fully respect the First Amendment guarantees, they assert the cults hide behind the First Amendment in order to shield themselves from criticism and legal restraint. They believe that while the First Amendment provides freedom for many different kinds of religious expression, it does not provide immunity when religious groups violate civil or criminal laws. They further believe the First Amendment provides freedom of religious thought but not freedom of religious action if such acts break the law. Religion in America is protected by the First Amendment but religion is not outside of or above the law.

They question whether freedom of religion is really at stake since "without freedom of thought there can be no freedom of religion," explains Joe Alexander, who heads a countercult group in Tucson, Arizona. Freedom of thought is based on freedom of choice, which in turn implies that decisions are made without psychological coercion or thought manipulation. Critics assert that a cult member may lose his ability to reason independently since he has been subjected to the cult's sophisticated coercive persuasion techniques. Also, the cults are often deceptive when trying to recruit new members and do not at first make known many crucial facts about the group. By the time the potential recruit is ready to make his decision to join he or she may no longer have the ability to think clearly enough to make the decision freely. Thus, says UCLA law professor Richard Delgado, "a convert never has full capacity and knowledge simultaneously."

In addition, some legal authorities believe the absolute guarantees of the First Amendment must be weighed against the cults' abuses such as invasion of privacy, blackmail, kidnaping, and starvation. Lawyer Robert Boetcher asserts: "We are witnessing a perversion of freedom of religion by cults which think they have special license to violate laws . . . First Amendment protection doesn't apply to the Unification Church because there have been violations of law." New York City constitutional lawyer Ephraim London, commenting on a court case involving the attempts of Lawrence and Jan Rogow to extricate their daughters, Elizabeth and Margaret, from a Manhattan cult called the New Testament Missionary Fellowship, in 1973, explained that

> The free exercise of religion is, of course, protected by the Constitution but where religious observances result in harm to society, they may be curbed. Examples are snake worship, beliefs opposed to inoculation, and from what I have been told, the practices of the New Testament Missionary Fellowship . . . State intervention in such cases is permissible, and in fact may be necessary.

Professor Delgado agrees that traditional religious freedom must be weighed against the cults' clear potential for violence and permanent psychological damage.

Using the Legal System to Counter the Cults

How can the legal system be more effectively used to counter the cults?

One of the major questions is the right of cult members to solicit funds without restriction from the general public. Cult critics are calling for new antisolicitation legislation and for strict enforcement of existing laws to curb fund raising by the cults. They demand that those raising money clearly identify themselves and their group. There have been many court cases in the past few years over the issue of whether a religious group is required to obtain a license to solicit money. The right of the Unification Church to solicit funds from the public has been upheld in Long Island, New York, Minneapolis, Minnesota, Las Vegas, Nevada, Virginia Beach, Virginia, and New Brunswick, New Jersey. In 1977 courts upheld the right of Hare Krishna members to solicit in state parks in Pennsylvania and in the streets of Sacramento, California. In April, 1979, two Krishnas sued the Arizona cities of Scottsdale, Mesa, and Tempe for violating their civil rights in passing restrictive solicitation ordinances.

In 1979 the North Carolina Court of Appeals ruled a state law unconstitutional that required religious and other organizations to obtain a license in order to solicit funds. The North Carolina laws applied only to those groups that obtain 51 percent of their contributions from nonmembers. The laws also gave the state the right to determine whether an organization used "an unreasonable percentage" of its income for other than "charitable purposes." The suits challenging the constitutionality of such laws were filed by the Unification Church and the PTL (Praise the Lord) Television Network of Charlotte, an Evangelical Christian group. In its ruling the North Carolina Court declared that the laws are "arbitrary and irrational" since they do not provide the state with adequate standards to make licensing decisions. Most importantly, the solicitation laws are, in effect, unconstitutional "prior restraint" because they give the state the right to decide whether certain religious activities are for a "charitable purpose." This, the court ruled, violates the First Amendment.

But in California the legal results have differed. In September, 1979, a Superior Court judge handed down a ruling that severely restricts Hare Krishna solicitation at the Los Angeles International Airport. Judge Robert L. Weil barred the Krishnas from touching "nonconsenting members of the public," putting cartons of literature near stairs or escalators, requesting donations repeatedly from people who have refused once, and claiming the money they are soliciting is for causes other than the Hare Krishna movement. In Georgia the fifth District Court of Appeals has upheld restrictions placed on Hare Krishnas at the Atlanta airport.

Historically, solicitation regulations have been left to municipalities, but fifteen states currently have legislation pending that would regulate solicitation by religious groups. The states are Alabama, Arizona, California, Colorado, Delaware, Indiana, Iowa, Missouri, New Jersey, Ohio, Oklahoma, Pennsylvania, South Carolina, Texas, and Vermont.

The entire question of solicitation needs further study. How can the legitimate rights of religious groups be fully exercised while at the same time protecting the general public from deception? What standards can be legally applied to a group that seeks to solicit funds in a public place?

Another important and highly complex issue is the right of the cults to claim tax-exempt status. The loss of that status would adversely affect them, and many critics are legally challenging the right of the cults to enjoy tax advantages. Sondra Sacks, an associate of Ted Patrick, urges full taxation of the cults. Her proposal has drawn sharp criticism from the cults as well as from traditional religious groups who fear their own tax-exempt status might be weakened or lost.

Under existing laws, the income and property of religious institutions are free of taxes as long as that income and property is directly used for specific religious purposes such as the maintenance of houses of worship, religious schools, and cemeteries. The business income that is unrelated to the exempt purposes is usually taxed. Such taxable income may derive, for example, from general book publishing and film making, the manufacture of goods, or the sale of services such as classes in computer programming or speed reading. Cult critics allege that many of the activities of the cults have nothing to do with religion and are simply business enterprises and so the profits from these activities should be taxed. In 1977, by a vote of four to three, the New York City Tax Board denied the Unification Church's claim for tax exemption on several church-owned properties worth over $2 million on the grounds that the property was being used by the church for other than "religious purposes." Unification Church officials appealed the ruling, asserting that the buildings had all been purchased for strictly religious activities. The case is still pending.

Other critics go further and charge that the cults are not even religions. Gifford Capellini, Jr., a Wilkes-Barre, Pennsylvania, lawyer who leads a deprogramming organization called Freedom of Mind, Inc., argues: "These groups have nothing to do with religion . . . They are pseudo-religious cults." The Unification Church has been accused of devoting major portions of its time and budget to political activities rather than to conventional religious programs. If it can be successfully proven that the Unification Church and other cults are in fact political groups posing as religious organizations, tax-exempt status could be withdrawn. Although it is dangerous to allow the government to decide what is and what is not a religion, it is clear that the political activities of some cults have not received sufficient attention and study by public officials.

Congressional investigators who probed the mass murders in Jonestown pointed out in their 782-page report to the House Foreign Affairs Committee in 1979 that Jim Jones's cult enjoyed "advantages and privileges" in its tax status even though the group had become "a sociopolitical movement." The Congressional group admitted that although the People's Temple

> may have been a bona fide church in its . . . early origins, it progressively lost that characterization in almost every respect . . . People's Temple was in the end a Socialist structure devoted to Socialism. Despite that fact, People's Temple continued to enjoy the tax-exempt status it received in 1962 under Internal Revenue Service rules and regulations. The issue of People's Temple . . . is also significant in connection with the First Amendment's protections it sought and received.

The House investigators called for some important tax changes. They recommended that

appropriate Congressional committees consider reviewing pertinent IRS rules and regulations . . . to provide for periodic IRS review of qualifying status in order to assure that originally stated purposes and objectives of the institution are still being fulfilled . . . also worthy of specific review is the procedure whereby exemptions are authorized under a "group ruling" to an association of churches when the members of the association may have little resemblance to each other in terms of doctrine or method of operation.*

(The People's Temple had been officially affiliated with the Christian Church—Disciples of Christ, a national Protestant denomination based in Indianapolis. Although it was a loose relationship that grew more remote each year, the People's Temple received and maintained a tax-exempt status under its 1962 "blanket ruling" with the Disciples. Since the Jonestown murders the Disciples have taken steps to increase the "shepherding" or supervision of its member churches through regular visits from the national leadership. More careful "shepherding" might help prevent another People's Temple situation.)

The Congressional Subcommittee headed by former Representative Donald Fraser that conducted an intensive investigation into the Unification Church in 1978 called for a Governmental Interagency Task Force to examine fully the church's record of compliance with a number of United States laws, including taxation regulations.

Health and sanitary codes should be more strongly enforced, especially against those groups whose members live together in crowded conditions. In addition to the corpse kept in Oric

---

*"The Assassination of Leo J. Ryan and the Jonestown Tragedy," U.S. House of Representatives International Relations Committee. May 15, 1979, U.S. Government Printing Office, Washington, D.C.

Bovar's apartment for over three months there have been other reports of unsanitary conditions in some cults. In 1978, New York City health officials evicted two hundred members of the Church of Bible Understanding, also known as The Forever Family, from the group's headquarters. They found them living in a filthy, rat-infested 2,000-square-foot loft with only two toilets and one sink and no bathtubs or showers. The two hundred men, women, and children had to use public baths in the Bowery. In *All Gods Children*, Stoner and Parke relate that one former member broke out with scabies all over her body during the six months she was in the Church of Armageddon. (Scabies, caused by mites that get underneath the skin where they lay eggs, is nurtured by conditions of malnutrition and personal uncleanliness.) Former Unification Church member Christopher Edwards asserts that in the eight months he was in the church there were many epidemics during which he saw "eighty or one hundred people lying on the ground vomiting." He believes these epidemics were caused by the fact that the Unification Church did not wash dishes with soap because using soap was "unspiritual" and "cost money."

Cult critics believe existing child-abuse and involuntary servitude (being forced to work for no wages) laws should be enforced against the cults to end the tragedy of alleged mistreatment of both adults and children. In August, 1979, New York State Assemblyman Howard Lasher's State Assembly Committee on Child Care held hearings on the treatment of children in religious cults. Annette Daum, Religious Action Consultant to the Department of Interreligious Affairs of the Union of American Hebrew Congregations and a member of the Task Force on Missionary Activity of the Jewish Community Relations Council of New York, testified that

> Former members of People's Temple have revealed that bizarre punishments were often inflicted on "rebellious" members, including physical and psychological abuse of children . . . teen-

agers received public beatings with paddles. Young children were subjected to electric shocks with a cattle prod or holding their heads under water at the bottom of a well for wetting the bed or stealing a candy bar.

Another group pairs off sixteen-year-old boys and girls in "small marriages," and, according to Mrs. Daum, subjects children "to brutal punishment for minor infractions, [being] beaten, kicked, forced to run until exhausted."

Christopher Edwards testified at the Lasher hearings that "since the Unification Church teaches that children born of marriages outside the cult life are children of Satan's world, they were generally treated with minimal care at best." They were often separated from their mothers. Edwards was not allowed to set up day-care centers for the children because the church leaders did not want to spend the money.

Edwards reports that by accident he stumbled across a small trailer in the California Unification Church farm where some six children were kept untended and in very crowded quarters. He believes that few in the church knew of their existence. The children did not even attend school. Next to their trailer, he testified, there was

another isolated trailer where adult members of the cult were housed without medical care when they became too ill to work. Children were constantly exposed to any illnesses from measles through a number of disorders caused by inadequate sanitary conditions. On at least one occasion when an epidemic on the farm was severe, adult members who were ill would be housed in the same trailer with these children.

Edwards agrees with other critics who believe that some cults seek to proselytize small children. He told the Lasher committee that while he was still an active Unification Church member, he planned to set up an elementary school in San Francisco, using a false name and false papers. Families who sent their children to the school would not know it was operated by the cult to convert their children and make extra income for the Unification Church. The standards, of course, in the school would be . . . unsupervised by people not tied to the cult. The children would be indoctrinated with the refinement and fine technology used in the training camps on the adults in the Unification Church.

Cult observers single out the Church of Armageddon for severe mistreatment of children. The FBI is studying reports that the Church of God and True Holiness, a Durham, North Carolina, group of sixty to three hundred members founded and led by the Reverend Robert A. Carr, practices involuntary servitude and child abuse. Members are forced to work for the cult, are not paid, and fed only one meal a day. Ex-members charge that children and adults are severely whipped and forced to fast for long periods.

Additional federal and state investigations and hearings such as those held by Assemblyman Lasher in New York should be conducted to determine whether or not some of the cults are violating human rights, including the right to proper diet, medical care, and protection from unlawful imprisonment, abduction of minors, and cruel and unusual punishment. At a 1977 meeting of the American Academy of Religion in San Francisco one of the participants called for a "blue ribbon commission" composed of academic, legal, medical, and religious leaders to probe the "many charges of human-rights violations carried out by the Unification Church against its members."

In the mid-1970s when the Unification Church carried out an intensive recruitment campaign on the streets of many American cities, observers noted the large number of Koreans, Japanese, and West Europeans who were part of that effort. Critics charged that the visas of some of these foreign cult recruiters had expired and consequently they were residing and working in the United States illegally. Representative Fraser's Congressional Report recommended that the Immigration and Naturalization Service fully enforce all immigration laws. This would help curb some Unification Church activities in this country as well as those of other cults which use foreign nationals as recruiters.

The Fraser Report also recommended that the Securities and Exchange Commission investigate the Unification Church's involvement with the Diplomat National Bank in Washington, D.C. to determine whether any federal banking or currency laws are being violated.

The bank has been a center of controversy since it was founded in December, 1975. A United States government investigation in 1976 charged that 50.8 percent of the bank's original stock was owned by foreign nationals (mostly Koreans with close ties either to the South Korean regime or to the Unification Church. Tongsun Park, a South Korean businessman and an alleged Washington influence peddler, was an early Diplomat National Bank stockholder.) However, United States law prohibits aliens from owning the majority stock of a federally chartered bank, and private investigator Galen Kelly claims that the aliens "divested" themselves of their majority holdings by turning their shares over to many young Unification Church members who were American citizens. These young people had donated their savings accounts to the Unification Church and received Diplomat National Bank stock in return. Kelly believes that the majority shares, technically owned by United States citizens, are, however, still controlled by Unification Church officials.

The United States Department of Labor has filed suit against the Tony and Susan Alamo Christian Foundation, charging the group with violations of interstate commerce regulations. The business activities of other cults involved in interstate commerce should be scrutinized as well.

Close examination of the cults' educational institutions has adversely affected some groups. In 1978, the New York State Board of Regents denied accreditation to the Unification Church's seminary at Barrytown. The Krishnas closed their elementary school in Texas rather than comply with changes ordered by the Texas Department of Education. Close monitoring of the cults' educational facilities should be continued. Some people believe that the cults should comply with strict consumer protection legislation. Julie Christofferson Titchbourne's important legal victory over the Church of Scientology in Oregon, in which she was awarded over $2 million, was filed under a consumer fraud statute. Critics hope that as a result of this case, other cults can be successfully fought in the courts on consumerism grounds.

Others advocate tightening laws regulating religious proselytizing. They suggest passing laws barring the conversion of minors. Annette Daum believes the legal age defining "minors" might be raised from eighteen years to twenty-one years in cases of religious conversion. There should be legislation forbidding proselytizing of wards of the state—many of the children killed in Jonestown were foster children, officially wards of the state—as well as people in mental institutions, hospitals, and prisons.

Laws insuring the proper education of school-age children should be enforced. Charity-fraud legislation might apply to some groups. New York attorney Patrick Wall who represents deprogrammer Ted Patrick believes some cults could be prosecuted under some states' laws which prohibit unjustifiable interference with familial relationships.

Preventive Remedies

Professor Richard Delgado asserts that the legal status of religious cults should be analyzed within the context of the Thirteenth Amendment of the United States Constitution—which forbids slavery—rather than within the First Amendment alone. He believes the conditions of some cult members do in fact constitute a state of slavery. Delgado has outlined the first comprehensive legal strategy offered to counter the cults. Writing in the University of Southern California *Law Review* in 1978, Delgado proposed six "preventive remedies" which are "aimed at regulating the private use of mind control by religious or pseudoreligious groups." He believes his remedies are "desirable" as long as they "provide adequate due process procedures and judicial oversight." His recommendations have stirred much spirited debate within the legal community.

Delgado demands that cults "identify themselves at an early stage and outline to the candidate what his life will be like" inside the group. Before a person joins a cult there should be a "mandatory cooling off period in which prospective members are required to leave the group . . . to reconsider their situation, and seek advice." This period of time would interrupt "the continuity of the [mind control] process." He calls for a public education campaign about the cults similar to present efforts to "discourage young people from smoking, drinking, and using addictive drugs." Delgado seeks a "flat prohibition of proselytizing by groups that utilize intensive psychological indoctrination," and he wants the state, through its licensing power, to "forbid unqualified individuals from engaging in psychologically intrusive practices." Finally, Delgado calls for a "living will" in which a person expresses the desire to be "rescued should he come under the influence of a cult."

Former Members and Others Sue the Cults

The cults are coming under legal attack from another quarter: former members. In the past, most ex-followers have been so stunned by their cult experiences that they sought only a quiet and tranquil return to society, and generally have avoided bringing law suits against the cults for alleged damages or for harmful acts committed against them. Simply grateful that their son or daughter had left the cult, parents wanted the whole unpleasant chapter closed as soon as possible. Parents and ex-members sometimes fear that any suit could result in a disastrous reencounter with the cult filled with ugly charges and countercharges and that a barely closed wound would be reopened. Some former followers who are still shaky even after deprogramming are afraid that renewed contact with their former cult, even in a courtroom setting, could end with their return to the group. Also, former members and their families are afraid that the cults might harass them if they battle them openly.

But this situation is changing. Former cultists are increasingly bringing many legal suits against the groups. In March, 1979, an Oregon court awarded former Unification-Church member, Christopher Rudie, $16,732 in damages because the cult failed to return his belongings after he was deprogrammed in 1976. Rudie, twenty-four years old, claims he "made $70,000 for them [the Unification Church] and they took all my personal possessions." Quadriplegic Timothy Goodwin sued The Way International and recovered money he had donated to it. Susan Murphy sued the Hare Krishna temples in Boston and Los Angeles for charges ranging from seduction of a minor to false imprisonment. A judge awarded former Children of God member Una Elizabeth McManus $1.5 million. An Oregon jury ruled in August, 1979, that the Church of Scientology must pay Julie Christofferson Titchbourne over $2 million in damages. These represent only a few of the cases being brought by former cult members.

Suits are now being brought against the cults by observers of the cult scene also. Peter Rudie, a lawyer who is Christopher Rudie's brother, is suing Scientologists in Oregon, claiming church officials libeled him. Some of the writers who have been sued by Scientology are now filing countersuits charging the group with harassing them.

Other Ways to Counter the Cults

In addition to the development of legal strategies, what other steps can be taken to counter the cults?

Parents of cult members have been in the forefront in alerting the general community to the cult phenomenon and in demanding full legal protection for cult members. Just a few years ago, however, many parents were passive when they learned that their son or daughter had entered a cult. A sense of guilt coupled with embarrassment often paralyzed them and kept them from taking action. Indeed, some parents denied that their child was even in a cult, claiming instead that "our Linda is in France attending an art institute" or "Richard is 'finding himself' in California" when, in fact, Linda and Richard were members of the Hare Krishna. Parents often possessed little or no accurate information about the cults and despaired of receiving any help or even understanding from public officials.

In the mid-1970s, some parents organized associations to exchange detailed information about the precise methods and ideologies of the various groups in order to offer mutual psychological support and to press appropriate leaders and officials for assistance. Some of the parental groups moved into the area of deprogramming. Today there is an extensive network of such organizations, and bewildered parents need no longer face the challenge of the cults alone. However, many parents still have difficulty finding out where to turn and whom to contact. Philip Cushman of the West Coast Jewish Training Project in San Francisco believes the anticult "network" should be better publicized and made more accessible to desperate parents.

One of the best-known groups is the American Family Foundation in Lexington, Massachusetts. K. H. Barney, an engineer at Raytheon Electronics, established the foundation because of his concern for those "persons and organizations which employ behavior modification or mind control techniques" and threaten the "rights of individuals and the integrity of the modern family." (A listing of countercult groups can be found on pp. 153-154.)

Guidelines for Parents

The parental groups offer some basic guidelines for helping parents cope with the cult problem:

1. Avoid severing communications with the family member

in a cult. A letter every six weeks or even every six months is better than no letter at all, and the same is true for telephone calls. The thread of communication between the family and the cult member, no matter how tenuous, must be maintained, if at all possible.

2. Try to get the cult member to come home for a visit even if he is accompanied by a "spiritual partner" who is another member of the cult. Family functions, holidays, even an illness, or a funeral are good excuses. Such visits will keep contact alive.

3. Avoid debating the cult's ideology, methods, or theology in letters, on the telephone, or in person. If a cult member who comes home for a visit is accompanied by one or more "spiritual partners," conversations between parents and child are not private. Long-distance telephone calls are also usually monitored by the cult and members who successfully resist the arguments of "satanic" parents are applauded by the other cult members for their loyalty. Even if a private conversation with the cult member is possible, a debate about the cult's ideas will be counterproductive. Concentrate instead on making the cult member feel wanted and accepted in your home.

Many members remain in a cult for several years. Thus, the parents should "settle in" for a long vigil. The cult member must know that the door of return to the family is never closed.

4. If a cult member does leave the group, do not attempt immediately to replace the cult experience with another religion. Many returnees express suspicion and wariness toward all religions following cult involvement.

5. A member needs time to be isolated from all cult contact after returning home. Sometimes a single visit or telephone call from a friend in the cult is enough to bring him back into it.

6. Because parents and other family members are emotionally involved with the cultists they are often ineffective in persuading them to leave a cult. Peer group members or former

teachers are more successful in this role, especially high-school or college friends who have chosen different religious paths. Just as peer group influence helps get a person into a cult, the same factor can help get followers out of it.

Also, former cult members who have struggled successfully to leave a cult and reenter society can give psychological support to the person attempting to leave a group. Countercult groups can put parents in touch with former cult members in the area.

7. Intense professional psychological counseling for a longer period of time may be necessary. Parents should seek help from a professional who has had experience with former cult members and their special problems.

What Are the Problems of Former Cult Members?

Psychiatrist Margaret Singer explains some of the problems former cult members face. They often find making personal decisions difficult, since the cult has been making all decisions for them. Many ex-cultists cannot make even small, unimportant decisions, so the task of planning for their futures can be a staggering one. Many "tend to sit and wait as they did within the group until things are suggested to them," says Dr. Singer.

Former members are often bitter and depressed over the lost years spent in a cult. Many young people entered the cult with a sense of innocence and naïveté. After leaving the group, they see all too clearly the hypocrisy of the cult leaders. Their "age of innocence" is gone forever.

Former members are often very lonely after leaving the group. They find themselves out of touch with people their own age. Gone are the "spiritual partners" and ready-made group of friends. The individual must now seek out new contacts and relationships on a personal basis, involving both initiative and decision making which he or she may now find difficult. The individual must also establish new and meaningful sexual relationships. Problems ensue because all sexual decisions were dictated by the cult, and the former member may have been traumatized by either sexual deprivation or sexual abuse in the group.

According to Dr. Singer, certain individuals may, after leaving the group, "slip back into the former states of consciousness," which were induced by the cult for months and even years. One former member who was in a cult for two years was exposed to countless hours of listening on a headset even in his sleep to tapes of the cult leader giving information and lectures. He recounts:

> For weeks after I left I would suddenly feel spacy and hear the cult leader saying, "You'll always come back. You are one with us. You can never separate." I'd forget where I was. I got so frightened once that I slapped my face to make it stop.

Some former members are afraid of harassment or persecution by people still in the cult. They relive the fear and humiliation they felt while in the group. One woman who had been in a cult for five years said:

> Some of the older members might still be able to get me and crush my spirit like they did when I . . . couldn't get out and fund raise or recruit . . . Then they made me crawl at their feet. I still freak out when I think how close they drove me to suicide that day . . . It was a nightmare.

Ex-cultists are sometimes embarrassed by their past cult experiences. "People say, 'How could you? You seem so nice and bright,'" Dr. Singer explains. They may have trouble being accepted into school or getting a job because they must either leave gaps in their applications for those lost years or confess to cult involvement. This often prejudices people against them.

Finally, Dr. Singer says, "ex-cult members have left an elite group . . . members are told they're going to change society and save the world, and coming back into the wider society they become just like all the rest of us." They face a great let-down.

Clearly, good professional rehabilitation and counseling are needed to assist the individual in reentering society. Philip Cushman's project is one new approach to the problem. He focuses his counseling process on the returning cult member's family, preparing it for what to expect when the child comes out of the group and how to cope with the problems afterwards. The former member is counseled within the context of the total family setting. Cushman reports great success in his efforts.

Cushman and others deplore the lack of willingness or the inability of the professional mental-health establishment, including those counselors affiliated with religious groups, to deal with the cult phenomenon and with former members. "They don't recognize the special mental problems created by the cults, and if they do recognize them they don't know how to deal with them," Cushman complains. "Professionals without a knowledge of these special problems can do more harm than good in counseling." Some Christian and Jewish groups have undertaken special counseling programs for cult returnees, but many more are needed. The entire mental-health community along with religious institutions must become more aware of the challenge of the cults and must equip themselves to treat cult victims.

Some cult observers echo Richard Delgado's call for an intensive public education campaign about the cults. Dr. Lester Rosenthal of the National Conference of Christians and Jews told the Lasher committee he believes ninth, tenth, and eleventh graders should be required to take courses in school on how the cults recruit and operate. A recent Gallup poll of American teenagers indicates that America's teenagers are ignorant about the cults—the poll shows that 59 percent are unfamiliar with the Unification Church and its teachings.

The new religious cults have presented some extraordinary challenges, but there are legal methods of combating them. Existing laws of conservatorship and *habeas corpus* are being used in new situations. Existing civil and criminal laws should be fully applied to the cults and new legislation and regulations enacted if necessary to counter any illegal activities. Close scrutiny must be given to the varied political and business activities of these groups to determine if any laws are being broken. Yet all of this must be done without sacrificing the two hundred-year-old American tradition of religious freedom guaranteed under the First Amendment.

Parents and other cult critics must be supported in their quest for legal action to protect cult members and to curb the cults. More professional help should be given to former cult members trying to readjust to society. In addition, parents need to accept the fact that by joining a cult their children have perhaps declared unhappiness with many parental values and beliefs. As part of their "open-door policy" parents should express a willingness to be flexible and to work with their children in shaping new patterns and styles of family life.

Finally, the single most critical issue must be fully addressed: cult members must have legal and safe means voluntarily to leave a cult. The right to leave a cult group must be as legally protected as the right to enter one.

Chapter 5

CAN CHRISTIANITY AND JUDAISM MEET THE CHALLENGE OF THE CULTS?

Obviously, the most effective way to counter the cults is to prevent people from going into them. Established religions and religious organizations can do much to answer the needs of those who defect to the new religious cults.

Future historians will give our generation high marks for some of our achievements in religious life. We will probably get an "A" for erecting impressive churches, synagogues, hospitals, counseling centers, homes for the aged, community centers, and for maintaining a huge multi-billion-dollar philanthropic network. We have built a vast educational system ranging from nursery school to graduate seminaries; many of our finest colleges and universities were founded by Christian and Jewish groups.

Historians of the future will also give our generation an "A" for our extensive system of religious communications—radio and television programs, publishing houses, magazines, tape cassettes, and newsletters—and an "A" for the sheer number of people in the United States who are affiliated in some way with a religious institution. The figure is over 150 million! This represents the single, largest membership group of any kind in the nation.

But the historians' grades will be quite low when they evaluate the little real spiritual substance found within our institutions. How much "God talk" really goes on inside our churches and synagogues? How often are true spiritual values stressed? What answer to the question, "Is that all there is?" does a person find in today's houses of worship? Does the 150 million figure dull our senses and make us forget the needs of the individual person who is lonely and in search of spiritual values? Are we guilty of playing the "numbers game," when it is the lone, alienated person who truly counts? The dramatic rise of the cults and their ability to attract new members clearly shows that if an individual cannot find an adequate spiritual response in the local church or synagogue, he or she will surely look elsewhere.

The traditional religious institutions need to become more flexible and to gear up to meet the challenge of the cults. Some cults offer coffee houses, short- and long-term counseling services, twenty-four hour emergency telephone "hot lines," hostels for travelers, and sometimes even career or school advice. All the cults promise a loving and caring community and a concrete way to improve the world. The traditional religions can do no less if they are serious about countering the cults.

People must be made aware of the rich variety of life-styles and religious options that exist within contemporary Judaism and Christianity. An individual can find direct, immediate religious experience in the joy of Jewish Hasidism or in the intense emotionalism of Charismatic Christianity. If he seeks more structure, regulation, and authority in his life he need not join one of the new religious cults.

We need smaller, more personalized religious units rather than the large, impersonal institutions that our traditional religions have provided over the past several decades. Especially in religion, bigger is not always better. One can become part of the underground church or a Jewish "chavurah" (fellowship) group, both committed to small group experiences and to spiritual renewal through experimental liturgies, communal study, and the joy of true fellowship. Such groups have experienced rapid growth during the last decade and they continue to gain new members, some of them former cult followers. These small pockets of religious energy function as extended families, offering a secure anchor in an uncertain and complex society. Such new directions in religious structure should be encouraged.

But ultimately the core of the long-term response to the cults must be increasing and deepening religious education on all levels. The cults appeal primarily to individuals who are unsure of or ignorant about their own heritage, or for whom their own heritage has meant little. Educational efforts must begin at the nursery-school level and extend upward to include substantial adult education. Junior and senior high-school students, especially, should be given a detailed cult "terrain map" to prepare them for coping with the agressive recruiting and proselytizing techniques of some of the groups. At a recent gathering of teenagers between the age of fourteen and nineteen in the West, eighteen out of forty reported that they had been approached by one of the cults, and over half knew of a friend who had been approached. We must arm this age group with information. Extensive training programs for teachers and youth-group leaders can sensitize them to the methods and ideologies of the various cults. Those individuals who have had firsthand personal experience with the cults should be utilized in this massive educational effort.

All evidence indicates that it is the home which chiefly transmits basic religious identity and belief. Rather than simply chauffeuring the children to Sunday school, parents also need to live out their commitment to religious values so that religious traditions become vibrant and alive for the family as a whole.

The established religions and religious organizations are finally reacting to the challenge of the cults, especially since the tragic events at Jonestown. These efforts must be continued. Until and unless the authentic and traditional communities of faith are strengthened, the exodus of searching people will continue.

SUGGESTED READING LIST

COHEN, DANIEL. *The New Believers: Young Religion in America.* New York: Ballantine Books, 1975.

CONWAY, FLO, and SIEGELMAN, JIM. *Snapping: America's Epidemic of Sudden Personality Change.* New York: J. B. Lippincott Company, 1978.

EDWARDS, CHRISTOPHER. *Crazy for God: The Nightmare of Cult Life.* Englewood Cliffs, New Jersey: Prentice-Hall, Inc., 1979.

ENROTH, RONALD. *Youth, Brainwashing, and the Extremist Cults.* Grand Rapids, Michigan: The Zondervan Publishing House, 1977.

HOROWITZ, IRVING LOUIS, Ed. *Science, Sin, and Scholarship: The Politics of Reverend Moon and the Unification Church.* Cambridge, Massachusetts: The MIT Press, 1978.

LIFTON, ROBERT J. *Thought Reform and the Psychology of Totalism.* New York: W. W. Norton and Company, Inc., 1961.

NEEDLEMAN, JACOB, and BAKER, GEORGE, Eds. *Understanding the New Religions.* New York: The Seabury Press, 1978.

PATRICK, TED, with DULACK, TOM. *Let Our Children Go!* New York: E. P. Dutton and Company, Inc., 1976.

STONER, CARROLL, and PARKE, JO ANNE. *All Gods Children: The Cult Experience—Salvation or Slavery?* New York: Penguin Books, Inc., 1979.

UNDERWOOD, BARBARA, and UNDERWOOD, BETTY. *Hostage to Heaven: Four Years in the Unification Church by an Ex-Moonie and the Mother Who Fought to Free Her.* Clarkson N. Potter, 1979.

WOOD, ALLEN TATE, with VITEK, JACK. *Moonstruck: A Memoir of My Life in a Cult.* New York: William Morrow and Company, Inc., 1979.

COUNTER-CULT ORGANIZATIONS

American Family Foundation
P. O. Box 343
Lexington, Massachusetts 02173

Citizens Freedom Foundation
Box 7000-89
1719 Via El Prado
Redondo Beach, California 90277

COPAC (Citizens Organized for Public Awareness Against
the Cults)
P. O. Box 3194
Greensboro, North Carolina 27402

Ex-Members Against Moon
P. O. Box 62
Brookline, Massachusetts 02146

Citizens Engaged in Freeing Minds
P. O. Box 664
Exeter, New Hampshire 02833

Freedom Counseling Center
1633 Old Bay Shore Highway, #265
Burlingame, California 94010

Free Minds, Inc.
P. O. Box 4216
Minneapolis, Minnesota 55414

Spiritual Counterfeits Project
P. O. Box 4308
Berkeley, California 94704

West Coast Jewish Training Project
190 Denslowe Drive
San Francisco, California 94132

Index

Adler, David, 124
Alamo Christian Foundation,
    Tony and Susan, 58-62,
    101, 136
  coercive persuasion in,
    60-61
  history of, 58-59
  income of, 59
  legal conflicts of, 61-62,
    136
  location of, 59
  marriage in, 60
  members
    and contact with outside
     world, 60
    living and working
     conditions of, 59-60
    number of, 58
    religious background of,
     101
Alamo, Susan, 7, 58, 59, 60,
    61, 62
Alamo, Tony, 58, 59, 60,
    61, 62
Alexander, Joe, 127
American Family
    Foundation, 140
American Jewish
    Committee, 9, 11, 34
Anctil, Joe, 66
Armageddon, Church of, 24,
    28, 68-72, 116, 133, 135
  children in, 70, 71, 135

deaths in, 28, 68
disciplinary methods in,
    70-71
drugs in, 71
food of, 71
history of, 69
income of, 69
indoctrination and coercive
    persuasion in, 71-72
life-style in, 69
location of, 69
marriages in, 69-70
members
  and contact with
    parents, 69
  health of, 71, 133
  number of, 69
  sexual mores of, 70
  suicide of, 71
  and treatment of
    women 70
  weapons and military
    drills in, 71

Back to Godhead, 48
Banoun, Raymond, 90
Barney, K. H., 140
Barnhouse, Donald, 73, 74
Bavis, Donna Seidenberg,
    121
Bell, Lois and Raymond, 58
Bell, Sharon, 57, 58
Bennetti, Angelo, 61

Berg, David Brandt
("Moses," "Mo"), 7, 75,
76, 77, 78, 79, 80, 81, 82
Berg, Sara, 81
Bergman, Michael, 63
Bible Understanding,
Church of (The Forever
Family), 133
Body of Christ, 72-74
beliefs and practices of, 73
children in, 74
coercive persuasion in, 74
disciplinary methods of, 74
family life in, 74
history of, 72-73
life-style in, 73
location of, 73
members, number of, 73
property of, 73
recruitment practices
of, 73
Boetcher, Robert, 27, 128
Bovar, Oric, 13, 15, 132-133
Boyle, Francis J., 126
Brownell, Bob, 60
Budlong, Morrison, 94

Canevaro, Emanuele, 79
Capellini, Gifford, Jr., 131
Carr, Robert A., 135
Cezares, Gabriel, 92
Children of God, 13, 24, 25,
74-82, 99, 100, 101,
122, 139
alcohol and drugs in, 78
and anti-Semitism, 75
beliefs of, 75

and Catholicism, 75
children in, 77, 78
and Christianity, 81-82
coercive persuasion
in, 80-81
history of, 76
income of, 79
legal problems of, 82, 139
life-style and living
conditions in, 78-79
location of, 76-77
marriage in, 78
members
number of, 76
religious background
of, 101
and "Mo Letters," 79-80
organization of, 77
and parents, 74-75,
81, 82
sexual practices of,
78, 80
spiritual counselors
in, 82
women in, 78
Clark, John G., Jr., 17,
27-28, 29, 90
Cobb, C. E. ("Buddy"), 72
Collegiate Association for
the Research of Princi-
ple (CARP), 35, 37
Conley, Harold, 45-46
conservatorships (guardianships), 20-121, 144
Conway, Flo, 5-16, 17, 52,
67, 89, 125
Cooper, Paulette, 90-91, 92

counter-cult groups, 38, 131, 140, 153-154
Cox, Edward and Patricia, 42-43
Cox, Harvey, 111
Crampton, Kathe, 70
Cults, the new religious:
 advertising and public relations techniques of, 16
 and anti-intellectualism, 20, 110-111
 appeal of, 105-117
 and blackmail, 22-23
 characteristics of, 20-26
 children in, 24, 28, 97, 102-103, 133-135, 137
 and Christianity, 19-20, 101-102, 106-108, 109-110, 112, 132, 144, 147-150
 and coercive persuasion, 16-18, 21-22, 125, 127-128, 143
 and consumer legislation, 137
 dangers of, 26-29
 defined, 14
 and the First Amendment, 82, 127-128, 129, 137, 145
 and guilt, 21, 22-23, 116
 and health and sanitation codes, 132-133
 in history, 14, 20
 and hypnosis, 17
 and Interstate Commerce violations, 136
 and Jews and Judaism, 101-102, 106-108, 112, 144, 147-150
 and the legal system, 119-122, 128-145
 locations of, 16
 number of, 14-15
 recruitment techniques of, 21, 127
 and religious pluralism, 26
 secrecy in, 25
 sexual mores in, 24, 112-113
 and solicitation regulations, 128-130
 and suicide, 28-29, 114-115
 tax-exempt status of, 130-132
 and violence, 25-26, 28
 wealth of, 18-19
 women in, 24, 28, 113
Cuneen, Mark, 61
Cushman, Philip, 38, 140, 144

Daley, William, 28
Daum, Annette, 133-134, 137
Davis, Maurice, 29
Davis, Rennie, 62
Delgado, Richard, 128, 137-138, 144
deprogramming, 8, 122-127
 dangers of, 125

effectiveness of, 123-125
history of, 122
legality of, 125-126
method of, 122-123
*Dianetics: The Modern
Science of Mental
Health,* 83
Diplomat National Bank,
41, 136
Divine Light Mission,
25, 50, 62-68, 100,
105, 123
alcohol, drugs, and
tobacco in, 63
children in, 64
food in, 63
history of, 62-63, 65-66
and hypnosis, 68
income of, 63, 66
Knowledge, dispensing
of 64-65
life-style in, 63-64,
66-67
location of 63, 66
Mahatmas of, 64, 66
meditation in 65, 67-68
members
number of, 63, 66
religious background
of, 101
Millennium '73, 65
obedience to Maharaj Ji,
67
recruiting techniques
of, 64
Satsang, 65
security force of, 25, 68

sexual mores in, 63
violence in, 68
Divine Principle, The, 32-34
Dole Hearings. *See* Informa-
tion Meeting on the Cult
Phenomenon.
Dole, Robert, 27-29

Edwards, Christopher, 22,
26, 39, 115, 124, 133,
134-135
End Time Ministry, The.
See Body of Christ.
Engle, Paul, 124
Enroth, Ronald, 70
Erdman, Paul. *See* Love
Israel.

Fabe, Barbara, 68, 123
Fabe, Linda, 123
Fife, Sam, 72, 73, 74
Ford, Alfred, 50
Forever Family, The. *See*
Bible Understanding,
Church of.
Foster, John, 95
Fraiman, Douglas, 72
Fraiman, Philip, 72
Fraser, Donald, 27, 41,
43-44, 132, 135-136
Fraser Report. *See* United
States Congressional
Sub-Committee on Inter-
national Organizations.
Filler, Tom, 124

Galanter, Marc, 15, 98-100,

102, 104, 105
God and True Holiness,
Church of, 135
Gonzales, Arlene, 61
Goodman, Malka, 92
Goodwin, Timothy, 57, 58,
139
Graham, Billy, 65
guardianships. *See* conserva-
torships.
Gutman, Jeremiah S., 120

habeas corpus, 121-122,
144-145
Hand, John, Jr., 67, 68
Hare Krishna. *See* Inter-
national Society for
Krishna Consciousness
(ISKCON).
Hargrove, Barbara, 116
Harrison, George, 49-50
Hassan, Steve, 37-38, 124
Heavenly Deception, 25, 40
Hebrew Christians, 9
Helander, Carolyn and
Elton, 121-122
Helander, Wendy, 121-122
Heldt, Henning, 94
Hermann, Mitchell, 94
Hill, Charlene, 73, 74
Hinson, John, 74
Holy Spirit Association for
the Unification of World
Christianity. *See* Uni-
fication Church.
Hubbard, Lafayette Ronald,
7, 83, 84, 85, 86

Hubbard, Mary Sue, 85-86,
94
Hunt, John, 82

Inchon!, 41
Information Meeting on the
Cult Phenomenon (Dole
Hearings), 17, 27, 29
International Conference on
the Unity of Science
(ICUS), 19
International Society for
Krishna Consciousness
(ISKCON) 18, 23, 25,
45-54, 99, 101, 106,
129-130, 136, 139, 140
chanting in, 47, 50, 52
children in 47, 51
clothing of, 18, 46
family life in, 47, 51
food of, 46-47
government of, 51
and Hinduism, 50
history of, 48-49
income of, 49-50
legal battles of 45-46,
53-54, 129-130, 139
location of, 48-49
marriage in, 47
members
health of, 51-52
number of, 48-49
religious background
of, 101
recruiting techniques
of, 51
security forces of, 25, 54

sexual mores in,
47
solicitation techniques
of, 51, 52-53, 54,
129-130
and suicide, 52
Transcendental Trickery
used by, 25, 53
treatment of women by,
47-48, 52
and weapons stockpiling,
54
Ishii, Mitshuharu, 41

Jeffers, Joseph, 13
Ji, Maharaj, 7, 50, 62-63,
64, 65, 66, 67, 68
Ji, Shri Hans, 62
John Paul II, Pope, 108
Johnson, Marolyn Lois, 65
Jones, Jim, 13, 26, 28, 68,
97, 98, 131
Jonestown. *See* People's
Temple.
Jordan, Fred, 76
Judah, J. Stillson, 101-102

Kaddafi, Moammar, 75
Kashian, Philip, 45
Kelly, Galen, 26, 45, 98-99,
102, 104, 105, 124, 136
Kember, Jane, 94
Killman, Marie, 91
Kirtanananda, Swami, 49
Kitch, Laura, 15
Kitchener, Bob, 58
Kitchener, Ida, 58, 60, 61

Kreshower, Edyth, 45
Kreshower, Merylee
(Murti Vanya), 45, 46

Larson, Barbara Anne, 121
Lasher, Howard, 133, 134,
135, 144
Leahy, John J., 46
Le Bar, James, 101
Lefkowitz Report, 76, 77, 78
Lifton, Robert Jay, 72, 109
Lloyd, Ellen, 39
London, Ephraim, 128
Love Family, The. *See* Arma-
geddon, Church of, 68-72
Love Israel (Paul Erdman)
68, 69, 70, 71

Mabry, Virginia, 45
McInnis, Ambrose, 110
McManus, Una Elizabeth,
139
McMurry, Gary, 89
Mahesh Yogi, Maharishi,
50
Manson, Charles, 71
Marks, Paul, 53
Master Speaks, 34, 44, 45
Mayer, Egon, 15
Meffen, James, 72, 73
Mick, Mrs. Chris, 60, 61
Mills, Jeannie, 21
Mishler, Robert, 67, 68
Moon, Sun Myung, 7, 21,
31, 32, 33, 34, 36, 37,
39, 40, 41, 42, 43,
44, 45

and anti-Semitism, 34
and Christianity, 33-34
life history of, 32
and mass weddings, 33,
  37
and North Korean govern-
  ment, 32
political activity of, 42-44
and ritual sex, 33
and South Korean govern-
  ment, 32, 43-44
and suicide, 44
as True Parent, 33
Mormon Church, 19, 20
Murphy, Angus, 45, 46
Murphy, Susan, 48, 51-52,
  53, 139

National Council of
  Churches, 33-34
News World 18, 28, 41
New Testament Missionary
  Fellowship, 128
New Vrindaban, 49
Nixon, Richard, 42-43, 108

Orlando, Joseph, 61

Paris, Joyce and Robert,
  70, 72
Paris, Tom, 70, 71, 72
Park, Chung Hee, 43
Park, Tongsung, 136
Parke, Jo Anne, 22, 81, 133
Patrick, Ted, 43, 70,
  122-124, 125, 126, 130,
  137

People's Temple, 8, 13-14,
  18, 21, 26, 28, 29, 68,
  97, 98, 102, 112, 119,
  126, 131, 132, 133-134,
  137, 150
deaths in, 8, 13-14, 18,
  26, 28, 97, 119, 126
discipline in, 133-134
membership of, 98, 102,
  137
tax advantages of, 131-132
weapons in, 26
wealth of, 18
Prabhupada, A. C. Bhaktivedanta, 7, 48, 50, 106-107
Prabhupada Place (Krishnaland), 49, 54
Praise the Lord Television
  Network, 129
Pugh, Idwal, 95
Pugliesi, Lawrence (Laxmi
  Nrshimha), 47

Rabkin, Judith and Richard,
  15
Raymond, Cindy, 94
Reichenbach, Edith von
  Thungen, 95
Reuther, Lisa, 50
Richey, Charles, R., 94-95
Robinson, Kenneth, 95
Rogow, Elizabeth and
  Margaret, 128
Rogow, Jan and Lawrence,
  128
Rosenthal, Lester, 144
Roszak, Theodore, 111

Rudie, Christopher, 139
Rudie, Peter, 139
Ryan, Leo, 26, 119, 132

Sacks, Sondra, 130
Salonen, Neil Albert, 32, 37, 121
Sapa, Church of. *See* Body of Christ.
Scales, Harold, 57
Schacter, Zalman, 21
Scheflin, Alan W., 120
Scientology, Church of, 82-96, 101, 137, 139
  beliefs of, 83-85
  blackmail in, 88-89
  and children, 85
  Citizens Commission on Human Rights of, 93
  and coercive persuasion, 88-90
  costs of, 85, 86
  disciplinary methods of, 88
  and family ties, 88
  and FBI, 91, 93-95
  and FDA, 93
  harassment of critics by, 90-92
  history of, 83
  legal battles of, 82-83, 87, 88, 89, 90, 91, 92, 93, 94-96, 137, 139
    in Australia, 95-96
    in England, 95
  location of, 83
  members

  number of, 83
  religious background of, 101
  working conditions of, 87
  mental effects of, 88-90
  National Commission on Law Enforcement and Social Justice of, 93
  and other religions, 85
  and processing (auditing), 84-85
  property of, 83
  recruitment methods of, 87
  and suicide, 90
  and violence, 91
Shapiro, Eddie, 45, 46
Shapiro, Eli, 46
Siegelman, Jim, 15-16, 17, 52, 67, 89
Singer, Margaret Thaler, 16, 90, 103-104, 124-125, 142-144
Siteman, Joseph, 28
Smith, Shari, 74
Snider, Duke, 94
Spero, Moshe Halevi, 22, 125
Stoner, Carroll, 22, 81, 133
Sullivan, Bob, 41
Swope, George, 104

Thomas, Sharon, 94
Titchbourne Julie Christofferson, 82-83, 87, 88, 89, 90, 91, 137, 139

Transcendental Trickery, 25, 53
Turner, Albert, 126
Turner, Shelly, 45
Tyce, Francis, 92

Underwood, Barbara, 124
Ungerleider, Thomas, 100, 102, 124
Unification Church, 18, 19, 20, 21, 22, 24, 25, 26, 27, 28, 31-45, 98, 100, 101-102, 104, 105, 115, 116, 120, 121, 122, 124, 126, 128, 129, 131, 132, 133, 134, 135, 136, 139 144
anti-Communism in, 42
anti-Semitism in, 34
children in, 134-135
and Christianity, 18, 33-34, 37, 101
coercive persuasion in, 34-38
food in, 36, 37
front groups of, 35
Heavenly Deception used by, 25
history of, 32
and hypnosis, 37
income of, 18, 39-41
and indemnity, 33, 34
and Jews and Judaism, 34, 101
legal conflicts of, 41-42, 43, 120, 121-122, 126, 129, 130-131, 132,
136, 139
location of, 31
and marriage, 33, 37
members
health of, 133
living and working conditions of, 31, 37, 38
number of, 32
religious background of, 101-102
and politics, 18, 41, 42-45, 131
recruiting techniques of, 21, 35-38, 135-136
sexual mores in, 33, 37
and suicide, 28, 45
theology of, 32-33
and violence, 25, 26, 28, 45
United States Congressional Sub-Committee on International Organizations (Fraser Report), 27, 43-44, 132, 135-136

Van Gorden, Kurt, 57-58
Vavuris, S. Lee, 120-121

Wade, Ron, 83, 89, 91
Wall, Patrick, 137
Wallisch, David, 124
Wasson, Jack, 80, 82
Way International, The, 26, 54-58, 101, 139
and coercive persuasion, 56-57

drugs in, 57
food of, 57
history of, 54-55
income of, 55-56
legal battles of, 58, 139
location of, 55
marksmanship classes in,
    26, 57
members
    number of, 55
    religious background of,
    101
    police force in, 57
    theology of, 56
Weeks, Lynn, 87
Weeks, Mary, 86, 87, 88-89
Weicker, Lowell, 41
Weigland, Richard, 94
Weil, Robert L., 53,
    129-130
Weiss, Leslie, 126
Wenderoth, Sandy, 59
West Coast Jewish Training
    Project, 38, 140, 144
Wheeler, Cheryl, 51
Wheeler, Devin, 51
Wierwille, Victor Paul,
    7, 54, 55, 56
Willardson, Gregory, 94
Wolfe, Gerald Bennett, 94
Wolfe, Tom, 109
Wood, Allen Tate, 39, 40,
    124

Yahwism, 13
Yanoff, David, 51
Yanoff, Jerry, 51